THE VIRGIN BIRTH
OF CHRIST

THE VIRGIN BIRTH
OF CHRIST

AN HISTORICAL AND CRITICAL ESSAY

BY

PAUL LOBSTEIN

PROFESSOR OF DOGMATICS IN THE UNIVERSITY OF STRASBOURG

Translated into English by

VICTOR LEULIETTE, B.-ès-L. (Paris), A.K.C.

Edited, with an Introduction, by

The Rev. W. D. MORRISON, LL.D.

Jesus said unto them: I am from above;
I am not of this world.—John viii. 23.

NEW YORK: G. P. PUTNAM'S SONS
LONDON: WILLIAMS & NORGATE

1903

Dedicated to

THE LATE

AUGUSTE SABATIER

PROFESSOR IN THE FACULTY OF THEOLOGY

OF PARIS

Introduction

In a remarkable letter which the Dean of Westminster has recently addressed to the Archbishop of Canterbury, he says: " No one will dispute the fact that in the minds of thoughtful men there is a very serious disquietude in regard to the doctrine of the Virgin Birth. It is only necessary, he continues, to ask any doctor, any student, of natural science, or any man who interests himself in scientific enquiries and their apparent conclusions, and endeavours to frame for himself a reasonable interpretation of the problems of life—to ask him not only what he himself thinks and feels, but what other men of his profession or class are saying to him, in order to discover that there is a real unsettlement

7

of their minds in regard to a matter which hardly occurred to their fathers as a subject of enquiry." The date of this unsettlement is, perhaps, rather more remote than the Dean supposes, but the fact of its widespread existence at the present moment, not only among thoughtful men, but also among scholarly theologians of the younger generation, is, as he truly says, not open to dispute.

What are the principal conditions which are producing this feeling of disquietude as to the character of the Christmas message? Undoubtedly one of the conditions is the general mental atmosphere which has been created among the educated classes by the spread of scientific habits of thought. Many people who are not themselves closely acquainted with either the principles or processes of scientific method have all the same unconsciously acquired a scientific attitude of mind, and it becomes exceedingly difficult for them to retain a place in their Christian consciousness for time-honoured beliefs which apparently run counter to their permanent habits of thought. It is, no doubt, possible to deal with individuals in this frame of mind by the Roman method of authority, and to demand of them a *sacrificium intellectus* as the price of remaining within the external organisation of the Christian Church. A disciplinary measure such as this will have the effect of producing silence, but it is impossible for it to produce conviction, and to silence the Christian conscience without convincing it is to sap the inmost foundations of the Christian life. In such a supremely sacred matter as Christian belief, force is no remedy, and the only way to remove difficulties from the path of faith is by removing the conditions which have been producing those difficulties. At the same time, it must be admitted that the conditions which are producing the present questionings with respect to the character of the Christmas message are, as far as we can see, likely to be permanent conditions: the rigorous exacting habit of mind created by modern modes of thought is

likely to be a permanent characteristic among
civilised communities : it is probable, in fact,
that this modern habit of mind will, with the
growth of education, ultimately pervade all
classes of the community, and become much
more dominant in the future than it is to-day.

Although the general mental atmosphere of
the times is one of the conditions producing
the existing unsettlement with regard to the
Christmas message, it is not the only or
perhaps the most important condition. During the last fifty years documentary criticism
of the New Testament has been making rapid
strides : the date, the historicity, the structure
of the New Testament writings have been subjected to minute, prolonged and searching
scrutiny, and although the outcome of these
scholarly investigations has been to establish
the general historic framework of primitive
Christianity, yet there are certain points on
which New Testament criticism has had to
speak with a somewhat halting voice, and one
of these points is the degree of historic value to

be attached to the miraculous events recorded
in the opening chapters of St. Matthew and St.
Luke. Are the most crucial parts of these
two chapters an accurate record of historic
events, or are they a phase of early Christian
theology cast into the form of a historic
narrative? Is the Christmas message theology
or history? That is the problem which New
Testament criticism has raised.

A great deal of uneasiness and misappre-
hension is aroused in certain ecclesiastical
circles by the fear that Biblical criticism is
raising the question of the inspiration of the
documents which contain the narratives of the
Infancy. That is a question which criticism
is not raising and which is beyond its com-
petence to raise. The inspiration of the Bible,
its religious saving value, is an entirely different
thing, and must always be kept apart from the
merely archæological question of the date,
origin, authorship, and structure of the books
of which the Bible is composed. The inspiration of the Bible is not in the least affected

by the results, whatever they may be, of
Biblical archæology. All that Biblical criticism can do is to compel us from time to
time to revise our conceptions as to the origin
and structure of the sacred documents, but
this revision of opinion does not diminish our
reverence for the Word of God which they
contain. The Inspiration, for example, of the
Creation narratives in the book of Genesis
is not diminished by the fact (now openly
acknowledged by all) that these narratives are
not a historic account of the actual order of
creation, but a theological presentment, cast
into a narrative form, of a belief in the divine
origin of things. The religious truth, the
inspiration, of the Creation narratives does
not consist in the cosmological conceptions
contained in these narratives: these cosmological conceptions are only the temporary and
transitory form in which the inspired writer
expressed his religious belief in the omnipotence
of the divine creative will. It is the religious
substance of the Creation narratives, and not

the temporary cosmological form in which they are cast, which constitutes their inspiration, and this eternal religious substance is entirely unaffected by the results of Biblical criticism, however radical these results may be.

It is possible and indeed probable that New Testament criticism may compel us to revise our traditional conceptions as to the physical background of the Redeemer's personality as it is represented to us in the two narratives of the Nativity; but as in the story of Creation, the religious substance of these two narratives is not their physical background but their expression of the religious belief that the Redeemer is the Incarnate Word, the supreme revelation of God. The form in which that belief is expressed in the narratives of St. Matthew and St. Luke may be historical or may be theological, but the religious truth of the belief itself is quite independent of the particular form in which it was expressed in early Christian times. The literal inspiration of the Bible, that is to say, the inspiration of the exact forms in which religious truth is expressed in Holy Writ, has been abandoned by all thoughtful Christian teachers as an utterly untenable position : the inspiration of the Bible is confined to its eternal religious substance, and does not extend to the external forms in which the Bible expresses religious truth. The particular form in which religious truth is expressed must always be relative to the age, if it is to exercise any effect on the hearts and minds of men : but a form of presenting Christian truth which is suitable to one age sometimes becomes unsuitable and inadequate to succeeding generations, and it is the supreme task of a theology which wishes to serve the highest interests of the Church to differentiate between the eternal substance of the faith and the temporary forms in which it must of necessity be expressed. A theology which is determined to tie down the Christian faith to the forms in which it was presented to the world at certain particular times is a theology which is bound to uphold the cosmology and the metaphysics of the ancient and mediæval world. It is enough to mention such a task to show its impossibility. We cannot go back to the forms in which the ancient and mediæval world expressed its conceptions of nature and reality; what we must do if we are to serve the Church of our time, is to divest the eternal truths of faith handed down to us by the past from the temporary envelope in which they are enclosed.

It seems to me that it is only by a theological method such as I have attempted to describe that we can approach acute questions of theology in the hope of ultimately finding a solution for them which will at once satisfy the demands of piety and truth. The mental temper of the age in which we live has an equal reverence for the facts of piety and truth, and the only way in which the theologian can meet the mental temper of the age is by presenting the facts of faith, so as to satisfy the twofold requirements of piety and truth. It is in this spirit that Professor

Lobstein endeavours to deal with the doctrine
of the Virgin Birth.   Opinions may differ, and
undoubtedly will differ, as to the conclusions
at which Professor Lobstein arrives in the
course of his enquiry, but it will be admitted
by all readers of this little volume that he
approaches his subject with a truly constructive purpose and in a fine Christian spirit of
candour, reverence, and sincerity.   Professor
Lobstein is not a voluminous writer, but he is
well known to all theological students, whether
in England or on the Continent, as one of the
most thoughtful and competent theologians of
our time.   It is to be hoped that the present
translation may be of service to many members
of the English Church who find insuperable
critical difficulties connected with the Nativity
as it is presented to them in the Gospel narratives.   Professor Lobstein's solution of these
difficulties is that the inspired substance of
these narratives should not be confounded
with the external forms into which it was cast
by the two Evangelists.   W. D. M.

Preface

THE following study, published first in French (1890), afterwards revised and enlarged in a German edition (1896), now appears in English for the benefit of English readers. The text itself has undergone no important changes; not so the explanatory notes and the bibliographical references. I was not only obliged to take notice of the publications which had appeared since the two preceding editions: it was specially incumbent upon me to take into account the English literature of which I had hitherto possessed but a scanty knowledge. I have tried to meet this need, although I dare not flatter myself that I have completely succeeded. Some of the names I met with are justly famed in English-speaking countries; I

have availed myself of the publications of
Bishop Gore and Dr. Sanday ; I have occasion-
ally discussed their opinions and objections.
Unfortunately the last book devoted to the
subject treated here only reached me when
the printing of my work was already finished.
It is impossible to pass over in silence the
recent book by Dr. B. W. Randolph.[1] Let
me devote my preface to this work, since it is
no longer possible for me to refer to it in the
body of my essay.

Dr. Randolph has made himself the staunch
and eloquent defender of the traditional
doctrine, but it cannot be said that he has
added a single argument to those adduced
hitherto by the supporters of the dogma. He
considers the matter briefly under four heads :
" First, I will try to give the evidence for the
belief in this article of the Creed during the
second century (3–22) ; next, I will ask you
to consider the evidence of St. Matthew and
St. Luke (23–34) ; thirdly, we will consider the

---

[1] *The Virgin Birth of Our Lord.* 1903.

argument *e silentio* on the other side (35–46) ; and lastly, I will ask you to reflect on the theological aspect of the question (47–57)."

After having collected the evidence of Ignatius, Aristides, Justin Martyr, Irenæus, Tertullian, Clement, and Origen, he concludes thus : " The testimony of these writers clearly shows that in the early part of the second century, and reaching back to its very beginning, the Virgin-Birth formed part of the tradition or doctrinal creed of the Church, and that this tradition was believed to be traced back to the Apostles " (18). In face of this accumulation of quotations one answer may suffice : the common source of all this patristic testimony is the double tradition contained in the Gospels of Matthew and Luke ; the *consensus* so urgently insisted upon by Dr. Randolph is accounted for by the fact that all the writers quoted went back to two of our canonical Gospels. But what follows ? Can this testimony avail to establish the credibility and historicity of our Gospels ? Not in the

least. The authority and probatory value of
the language of the Fathers is gathered only
from the two Gospel sources whence it proceeds; round these, therefore, the discussion
finally centres.

This is so evident to Dr. Randolph that in
his second chapter he treats of the Gospels of
Matthew and Luke. " Luke, he says, carries
us back into a world of religious beliefs and
hopes which clearly reflect and express a conception of the Messiah, naïve as yet and
elementary, and much earlier than the expan-
sions of the Christology of the Apostles; the
primitive character of the religion current
among the pious families of Israel vouches for
the historical accuracy of these narratives, the
tradition of which finally goes back to the
Virgin herself; this tradition was received and
set down by Luke, whose prologue witnesses
to his scrupulous exactness and high ability."
What remains of this fabric of affirmations,
by turns gratuitous, plausible or certain ?   That
the Evangelist was working upon older sources,

and that these sources originated in Jewish-Christian circles. Cautious criticism can go no further, without exceeding the limits imposed by the documents themselves.

Dr. Randolph seems to me especially weak in the way he states his questions. He affirms, for example, that this tradition of the Virgin-Birth cannot be " the work of forgers " (34. *Cf.* pp. 25–27). Such an assertion proves that he has not advanced very far in the psychological and historical apprehension of the formation of religious myths:—as being the spontaneous outcome of popular imagination, and not the reasoned invention of forgers and impostors. The aversion with which he looks upon the latter explanation—a puerile explanation, to which sane criticism has long since done justice—leads him to forge for himself or at least to adopt romantic explanations, which he tries to defend by means of distinguished names, without thereby successfully establishing their certainty. St. Joseph, he says, following in this the conjecture of Bishop

Gore (*Dissertations on Subjects connected with the Incarnation*, London, 1896[2]), had drawn up a detailed account of all the circumstances of the birth of Jesus ; after the death of Joseph, which took place before the public ministry of Jesus, this document passed into the hands of Mary, who could have used it, had occasion demanded, " to vindicate her own virginity " ; after Pentecost, Mary gave this explanatory document to the family of Joseph, the now believing brethren of the Lord ; these, finally, transmitted it to the author of the Third Gospel.   Truly, we may well be astonished at the ease with which the author bases on such conjectures a dogma which he proclaims essential and which he sets forth as one of the pivots of the Christian faith.

Our astonishment is still further increased by statements such as the following : " That there are differences and even discrepancies between the two accounts, which are manifestly independent of one another, serves surely to strengthen their witness to the great central fact in which they are at one—that Christ was born of a Virgin-Mother at Bethlehem, in the days of Herod the King (38). What! the differences, the discrepancies even, which exist between the two traditions are of such little moment, and are incapable of lessening the historical character of either the one or the other! Nay, rather, they actually furnish a striking confirmation of the grand central fact about which the two documents are in agreement! But, pray, how can two documents, both of which are individually far from trustworthy, ever attain, by simply being joined together, that cogency which separately they lack? how can they thus secure that assent which singly they are incapable of producing?

For the explanation of the origin of the Gospel story I venture to refer the reader to Ch. III. of the present study, which I hope will dispel the objections stated by Bishop Gore and Dr. Randolph.

The third chapter of the book I am trying to appraise searches out the causes of the

silence which the sacred writers have maintained respecting the miraculous birth of the
Saviour. Their silence neither perplexes nor
astonishes Dr. Randolph. For, after all, the
dogma of the Virgin-Birth was not at the
outset the subject of the preaching of the
Apostles ; it is neither the starting-point nor
the foundation of the Christian faith, it is only
the crowning of the edifice, the end reached by
the piety of the primitive Church. Is it not
the fact that here, as elsewhere, the author is
easily satisfied and reassured ?   How is it that
he does not perceive that he is proving more
than is necessary, or rather that his proof may
be turned against his own position ? If the
Virgin-Birth forms no part of the essential
truths preached by the Apostles, is it not clear
that the dogma is thereby singularly compromised ?   Have we not a right to conclude
from Dr. Randolph's own words that this so-
called divine doctrine is a late addition to the
sum of the testimony of the Apostles, a super-
added element in the Christianity preached in

its fulness by Paul and John, who neither of
them ever referred to the precise mode of
Christ's entrance into the world? And, in
fact, Weizsäcker in his classical work on the
Apostolic Age has not devoted a single line or
word to the tradition of the miraculous birth.
So true is it that, on the avowal of apologist
and critic alike, this tradition is foreign to the
missionary preaching and religious teaching of
the Apostles!

In his last chapter Dr. Randolph examines
the religious value and dogmatic necessity of
the Virgin-Birth. His examination rests upon
the constant confusion of three or four notions
originally and essentially distinct; the sinlessness of Christ, His Incarnation, His Divinity,
the fundamental difference which separates
Him from sinners. Nothing could be more
fatal and misleading than such a confusion;
nothing more elementary and superficial than
the following summary statement: if Jesus
Christ was not born of a Virgin, He is not the
Son of God, He is not the Saviour, He is not

sinless. That the unsophisticated layman should thus argue, is conceivable; but such a confusion seems hardly credible in a theologian. What! the new creation in the bosom of humanity, that creation which established Christ as the second Adam, the head of the Kingdom of God, necessarily involved the exclusion of a human father, at the moment of the conception and birth of the Saviour? What! we may not believe that Jesus Christ was born from above, without subscribing to the narratives of Matthew and Luke ? In the following study I have tried to break through the artificial link which unites these assumptions. The connection which some establish between religious truths of the highest importance and certain narratives in the Gospels of a doubtful historical character is attended by dangers of so grave a nature, that in the name of religion itself we must protest against mistakes and confusions condemned alike by sane criticism and religious faith. Similarly, the assimilation of the supernatural birth to the

resurrection of the Lord (pp. viii.–ix. *Cf.* pp.
1, 53) is not less arbitrary, besides being con-
tradicted by the unanimous testimony of the
New Testament—that is to say, by the primitive affirmations of the Christian consciousness.

Such, then, is the study recently published
by Dr. Randolph. It is based to a large extent
upon the first of Bishop Gore's dissertations
mentioned above; it reproduces and popular-
ises the latter's results. If the arrangement
adopted by Bishop Gore is different (§ 1.
The silence of St. Mark, St. John, and St.
Paul. § 2. The narrative of St. Luke. § 3.
The narrative of St. Matthew. § 4. The
relation of the two narratives. § 5. The
tradition of the Churches. § 6. The theory of
legend. § 7. The connexion of doctrine and
fact), if the critical apparatus in his work is
richer and stronger, the method and spirit of
the two authors are the same. In the course
of the following study I shall frequently be
obliged to take up arms against the learned
and pious commentator of the dogma of the

Incarnation. He is to-day, in England, the worthiest and most eminent exponent of the traditional doctrine. I confidently hope that, should he glance through this study, he will easily be convinced that my aim has been to set forth the religious and permanent value of the tradition of which he has made himself the defender, so that in the matter of piety, of faith, and of the eternal Gospel, concord between us will not only be possible, but even deep and intimate.

P. LOBSTEIN.

Contents

Contents

Contents

Contents

Contents

Contents

Contents

Contents

PAGE

popular symbolism of the Gospel myth.—Analysis
of the primitive and irreducible elements of
Christian experience.—Disadvantages and dangers of the official dogma : it fails to recognize
the essential nature of the Gospel revelation and
the inner character of the Christian faith, it im-
pairs the religious idea of the divinity of Christ
and the moral idea of His humanity, it rests upon
a primitive and superficial dualism between the
world of nature and the sphere of the supernatural.

VI

RETROSPECTIVE SURVEY AND GENERAL CONCLUSIONS, . 110

NOTES, ... 113

The Virgin Birth of Christ

I

" Ye are from beneath ; I am from above :
ye are of this world ; I am not of this world "
(John viii. 23). The believer who examines
his natural heart in the light of the Christian
revelation, finds in this declaration of the
Johannine Christ, at once so peremptory and
so absolute, the expression of his own inmost
experience of the person and work of Christ.
So deep is the gulf which separates him from
the One in whom he has found his Master and
his Saviour, that such a difference of nature
leads him instinctively to infer a difference of
origin. Thus the tradition of the miraculous
birth of Jesus seems to anticipate the conviction of the believer, merely transferring into

the realm of history a truth of which he finds in himself the most conclusive confirmation. And so he is not surprised that Scholastic theology, encouraged by the Church, should have raised the Gospel tradition to the rank of a dogma, sanctioned by divine authority.

Indeed, in the eyes of a considerable number of sincere and enlightened Christians, the story of the supernatural birth of Christ is an integral and essential element in the dogma of the person and work of the Saviour.[1] Sacrifice the belief in this miracle, they say, and you sap the very foundation of faith in the divinity and sinlessness of Jesus Christ. Some theologians[2] go so far as to attach little importance to the speculative thesis of the eternal pre-existence of the Word, yet assert, all the more vigorously, the dogma expressed in the so-called Apostles' Creed: "I believe in Jesus Christ, who was conceived by the Holy Ghost, born of the Virgin Mary."[3] This

---

[1] See Note I., p. 113.   [2] See below, § IV.
[3] See Note II., p. 113.

affirmation seems to them the necessary foundation of the divine life of Christ, and the indispensable condition of His work of redemption. They are ready to concede that the idea of the eternal existence of the Logos is a metaphysical notion beyond the reach of the human mind; but they think that the miraculous birth of Jesus, hallowed by the most touching and intimate of our Christian festivals, is a concrete fact, a positive and living reality, a story which speaks to the consciences and hearts of believers in simple, yet thrilling accents, full of sweet poetry and lofty eloquence. Surely the critic who rashly dares to handle this dogma, the mysterious and sacred keynote of the Christmas Gospel message, or the historian who analyses and discusses, where the believer blesses and adores, must be guilty of sacrilege and blasphemy!

There is nothing surprising in such a judgment. We should indeed be exhibiting naïve levity and gross lack of intelligence were we to attribute such a summary condemnation to routine alone, to the tyranny of inveterate habit or of dogmatic prejudice. No, the unconquerable antipathy which, in these matters, sceptical analysis causes to the confidence of piety, the antipathy which finds expression in indignant or sorrowful protest, is the outcome of a perfectly legitimate feeling, nay more, of a thought which is both just and true.

Let us reiterate, in order to remove all misunderstanding : the dogma or story of the "nativity" has it roots deep down in the soil of the Christian consciousness, and is the translation of a religious interest of the utmost importance. Any contribution to Christology which did not seek to safeguard this interest and to do it full justice, any solution which did not take into account the urgent needs of Christian piety and experience, would be finally condemned by every living theology, loyally interpreting the faith. To unravel and define the religious postulate which lies at the back of the double narrative of Matthew and

Luke, to defend its sacred and unquestionable authority, such is the chief task of the dogmatic theologian in presence of the incomparable traditions which shed their divine lustre around the cradle of the Saviour. The whole question of the story of the miraculous birth of Christ finally resolves itself into the following: Is the profession of the Christian faith, which supplies the sinew and gives its value to the Gospel tradition, bound up with the historic form consecrated by that tradition? In other words, does the witness which the Christian consciousness bears to the sinlessness of the Saviour, to the divinity of His character, to the redeeming efficacy of His work, also bear on the precise mode of His origin and sonship? Does the Christian's faith in Christ imply a settled opinion concerning the birth of Jesus? Such is the problem I wish to attempt to answer.

I confidently trust that the sincerity of these investigations will afford the best proof of the essentially constructive purpose which inspires and sustains them.   The most obdurate reader will, I hope, feel that criticism is for me a means only and not an end, and that my sole endeavour and only ambition are to lay bare the real and living kernel of the Christological dogma, with a view to carefully gleaning and strenuously safeguarding the religious and imperishable essence of the Christian faith.[1]

II

AT the very beginning of our study we meet with an objection, the importance of which cannot fairly be denied : we may perhaps be accused of having wrongly stated the question. " For, after all, we might be informed that we are dealing here not with an experience of the Christian consciousness, but with a fact of the Gospel narrative.   The point at issue is not a postulate of religious faith, but a datum of our Scripture records.   The discussion centres round the authority of Biblical testimony, not round the value of an assertion of experience.

[1] See Note III., p. 115.

You are removing the problem out of its proper place, if you raise it to the plane of dogma; you must confine it within the limits of exegesis and historical criticism."

Let us accept the question formulated in the above terms and examine the objection on its own ground. The position thus defined is very favourable to the advocate of tradition who maintains plenary inspiration. It is evident that if the narratives of Matthew and Luke were written under the immediate dictation of the Holy Spirit, they participate in the infallibility of divine inspiration; if human activity is altogether dispensed with in the composition of our sacred books, all possibility of error or inaccuracy is likewise precluded; there is no room in our supernatural documents for the smallest element of myth or legend; the data contained in our canonical Gospels must be taken in a literal and material sense; they are just as historical as the ministry in Galilee or the last week in Jerusalem. In that case any further discussion is both useless and blasphemous; criticism resolves itself into the purely external task of harmonizing, and the skill of the historian consists in the ability which he exhibits in arranging and fitting together the various materials of the Gospel narrative.

It seems to me unnecessary to linger over a point of view which, in theory at least, is rejected by all thoughtful theologians. No one to-day persists in maintaining the verbal inspiration theory of Gaussen and of the theology of the Revival. All contemporary exegetes and dogmatists are agreed upon "restoring its character to human activity." [1] It is, therefore, not only lawful, but necessary, to compare the accounts, to weigh the evidences and to criticize the sources.

What is the historical value of the documents which tell us the story of the conception of Jesus in the womb of a virgin and of His

---

[1] GODET, *Revue Chrétienne*, 1882, p. 714. The Revival was a pietist movement in French and Swiss Protestantism which arose in the early part of the nineteenth century.

miraculous birth at Bethlehem? When reduced to such proportions, the question is a
simple one and easily solved. We know that
the Protevangel is found in only two of our
Gospel narratives. Whatever we may think
of the historical trustworthiness of the two
first chapters of Matthew and Luke, we cannot
doubt that, in the minds of the Apostles and
of the two first generations of Christians, the
life of Jesus began at the baptism of John
and ended at the resurrection (Acts i. 22; x.
37; xiii. 24). Mark, who most faithfully represents primitive tradition, bears no sign
whatever of the gospel of the birth and childhood of Jesus.[1] Such an *evangelium infantiæ*
was no part of the first missionary and apostolic
preaching.[2] Further, it has often been pointed
out that, even in the Gospels of Matthew and
Luke, these two chapters do not form part of
the main body of the narrative, and that the

[1] A. SABATIER, *Quelques réflexions à propos du premier
verset de l'Evangile de Saint-Marc. Cf.* THRAEN, *op. cit.,*
p. 56 *et passim.*
[2] See Note IV., p. 118.

solution of continuity is so marked that it may well be asked whether they were not a later addition.[1] Under these circumstances, it is not surprising that criticism, finding itself on insecure ground, should show distrust and formulate rigorous and definite demands.

A more minute examination yields no more reassuring result. The narratives of the supernatural birth belong to a body of traditions which must be cautiously handled. The most superficial of readers easily perceives that the narratives of Matthew and Luke differ very materially in character, that they are not dominated by the same preoccupations and religious interests. The two traditions clearly arose in different environments and independently of each other. On this point all are agreed. But our two Gospels are not only different, they are contradictory. It is not enough to assure us that both cycles of narratives existed for a certain time, the one,

[1] A. SABATIER, *Encyclopédie des sciences religieuses* (Art. Jésus-Christ), vii. 363.

that of Matthew, as a public tradition coming
from Joseph, the other, that of Luke, as a
family remembrance treasured up by Mary[1];
for where they differ is not only in general
point of view, but in the very facts and in the
bond that unites them. It is impossible to
reconcile our two traditions without doing
violence to the texts, without resorting to
arbitrary hypotheses, and without resting
content with possibilities which will never
amount to historical certainty. Need I recall
the fact that the two genealogies reckon a
different number of generations, and that they
agree in only two names?[2] that the scene of
the annunciation in Luke is quite unlike that
in Matthew? that the double indication as to
the abode of the parents betrays an insoluble
contradiction? that the visit of the Magi and
the flight into Egypt, as related by Matthew,
cannot be fitted into Luke's narrative, either

---

[1] GODET, *Commentary on the Gospel of St. Luke,* i. 202–203.
W. SANDAY, *art. cit.,* pp. 65, 66, 68–69.   GORE, *op. cit.,* p. 78.
[2] See Note V., p. 119.

before or after the presentation of Jesus in the Temple? Nay more; not only do our two traditions mutually exclude each other, even when taken separately they raise insuperable difficulties. Traditional theology has been keenly alive to these difficulties, and the expedients to which it has resorted afford a sufficient proof of its perplexity; the rationalism of our modern orthodoxy transforms the miraculous star which went before the Magi into an astronomical conjunction or a phenomenon of the atmosphere; it does not shrink from "philological enormities and wild extravagance[1]" in order to make Luke mean something different from what he says about the enrolment under Quirinius; it attenuates or sets aside the miraculous intervention of the angels by reducing the sublime and naïve marvels in the accounts of Luke and Matthew to merely artificial processes of literary composition[2]; in

[1] REUSS, *Hist. évangélique* (Synopsis of the first three Gospels), 1876, p. 141.

[2] Such especially is the opinion of WEISS in his *Life of Christ* (Bk. I. ch. 1–5).

a word, in spite of the reverence which it pays to the sacred text, it does not respect its original meaning, but ignores its true character.

Will it be argued that the supernatural birth, given by two traditions manifestly independent of each other, gains from such a double witness, if not a complete confirmation, at least a presumption almost amounting to a certainty? Such a proof would be more specious than solid. Will two documents, each of which is seriously compromised, ever acquire, by being added together, that convincing force which individually they lack, will they ever furnish that evidence which separately they fail to offer? Further, what will happen if, in these very sources to which we are bidden to turn, we find indications which tell against the tradition and reveal a different outlook from that of our Evangelists?

The most striking indication is that furnished by the two genealogies preserved by Matthew and Luke.[1] Their object is to prove that Jesus

[1] A. Réville, *Histoire du dogme de la divinité de Jesus*

is truly the Messiah, by recording the succession of His ancestors in direct line from King David to Joseph, the husband of Mary. It is beyond dispute that in the mind of both genealogists Jesus is the son of Joseph. Had they possessed the slightest notion of a miraculous birth, they would have drawn up the genealogy of Mary, not of Joseph. Every artifice, M. Réville very ably says, every artifice resorted to by the old commentators to conciliate this contradiction in the Gospel records crumbled before the stubbornness of the texts. Our Evangelists evidently found these genealogies in older documents; then, because of the dearth of traditions current about the childhood of Jesus, they dared not reject any of those which came to their knowledge, but pieced together the little they collected about this obscure subject, of which Jesus himself had never spoken. This is the explanation

Christ, Paris 1869, pp. 25–27. The difficulties and contradictions alluded to here have been repeatedly pointed out by authors who cannot be accused of theological radicalism (*e.g.*, BEYSCHLAG, *Das Leben Jesu*, i. 164–165).

of the astonishing fact that the same Gospels
which have embodied these genealogies are
precisely those which relate the story of the
miraculous birth of Jesus. Matthew, who
places the two contrary traditions side by
side, seems to have attached to the historical
and natural genealogy a theocratic value which
furnished him with the solution of the difficulty; the sequel of Matthew's narrative,
according to which Joseph acknowledged
Mary's child to be his own, plainly shows us
that Joseph legally transmitted his hereditary
nobility, his real title of Son of David to one
who did not naturally inherit it.[1]—Luke, who
also intends to note down the genealogy of
Joseph the carpenter of Nazareth, born of the
seed of David (*cf.* i. 27 ; iii. 23), felt the contradiction, but tried to diminish, if not to annul
it, by prefacing the genealogical list with these
words : " Jesus was supposed to be the son of

[1] Reuss, *op. cit.*, pp. 118–119. *Cf.* A. Sabatier, *Généalo-
gies de Jesus-Christ* (Encyclopédie des sciences religieuses,
v. 464–466).

Joseph, the son of Heli. . . ." The historical books of the Old and New Testaments are full of examples of a similar welding together of various older documents, and apologists should be the last to denounce the primitive and absurd methods attributed to the sacred writers[1] by modern criticism; unless we are to apply to Biblical historiography a totally different standard of measurement from that warranted or required by the whole of antiquity, we cannot close our eyes to facts which an impartial reader meets with a thousand times over in our canonical writings.

This hypothesis is moreover confirmed by other details to be noted in the Gospels and even in the cycle of traditions concerning the infancy of Christ. The only feature of the childhood of Jesus reported by Luke forces us to conclude that the story of the first visit of Jesus to the Temple differs in origin from the Gospel of the miraculous birth. After having related the answer of Jesus to Mary:

[1] GODET, *op. cit.*, i. 203.

"Wist ye not that I must be in my Father's house?" the Evangelist adds: " They understood not the saying which he spake unto them" (Luke ii. 50). Is it not plain that Luke is here recording a tradition formed in a circle where nothing was known of the miraculous scenes, which, according to the same Evangelist, had accompanied the birth of Jesus, and the import of which Mary, at all events, could certainly not mistake?[1]

Still more unintelligible is the attitude of the mother and of the family of Jesus, during the course of His public life and during His Messianic ministry. One scene, of which Mark alone tells us the time and place, and the particular circumstances of which the other synoptists either ignore or pass over in silence, is still harder to reconcile with the "protevangel" than the details culled from Luke. The near relatives of Jesus, troubled at the excitement which is growing around His person and at the unusual character of

[1] See Note VI., p. 120.

His ministry, which appears to them more and more extravagant and eccentric, wish "to lay hold on him: for they said, he is beside himself." [1] When they arrive, He has just dismissed His adversaries, so that His mother and His brethren find Him in the midst of an audience eminently well disposed towards Him. "And they said unto him: Behold, thy mother and thy brethren without seek for thee. And he answered them saying: Who is my mother and my brethren? And looking round on them which sat round about him, he said, Behold my mother and my brethren. For whosoever shall do the will of God, the same is my brother, and sister, and mother." [2] We may attenuate or limit as much as we will the words of Jesus, [3] we may refuse to believe that He broke with His family or that He meant to upbraid His parents for their incredulity, it will nevertheless remain true

[1] Mark iii. 20–21 (see HOLTZMANN, *Hand-Commentar zum Neuen Testament*, 1889, p. 136).

[2] Mark iii. 31–35; Matt. xii. 46–50; Luke viii. 19–21.

[3] As does also REUSS, *op. cit.*, p. 290.

that the solemn declaration of Jesus, subordin-
ating family ties to higher and more enduring
ones,[1] was called forth by the fears of Mary
and of His brethren.

These fears would be absolutely inconceiv-
able were it true that Mary was piously
treasuring, as a family tradition,[2] the lively
remembrance of the scenes of the annunciation
and of the nativity.[3]

Nor shall we find when we pass from the
Synoptic Gospels to the other writings of the
New Testament any clearer evidence or even
any faint indications of the miraculous birth of
Christ.

The apostle Paul seems positively to ignore
the dogma. He does not require it to establish the sinlessness or the divinity of Christ.
Whether Paul is speaking of the Saviour's
entrance into the world and of His mission
from God, or whether he is insisting on the
fact of His perfect sinlessness, he nowhere

[1] GODET, *op. cit.*, i. 378.   [2] GODET, *op. cit.*, i. 202–203.
[3] See Note VII., p. 121.

alludes to the tradition consecrated by Matthew and Luke.[1] Two passages even seem rather to exclude than to imply the idea of the miraculous birth. The expression used by the apostle, in the introductory words of the Epistle to the Romans, to denote the human origin of Christ would be singularly inappropriate if Jesus had not come into the world in the ordinary way: the Son of God was born of the seed of David[2] according to the flesh (Rom. i. 3); yet, besides the σάρξ, Christ had in Him the divine power of the πνεῦμα, of "the Spirit of holiness," an essential feature in the personality of the Lord, whose divine sonship was declared and proved by the resurrection, not by the incarnation.[3] The following passage is still more explicit, "When the fulness of the time came, God sent forth his

---

[1] Rom. viii. 3 ; 2 Cor. v. 21.

[2] Ἐκ σπέρματος Δαυίδ κατὰ σάρκα. *Cf.* Gal. iii. 16 : Τῷ σπέρματί σου, ὅς ἐστιν Χριστός.—Rom. iv. 13 : ἡ ἐπαγγελία τῷ Ἀβραὰμ ἢ τῷ σπέρματι αὐτοῦ.—*Cf.* Rom. ix. 5 : ἐξ ὧν (πατέρων) ὁ Χριστὸς τὸ κατὰ σάρκα.

[3] See Note VIII., p. 122.

Son, born of a woman, born under the law"
(Gal. iv. 4). The being born of the woman
is here called by that name in order that He
may be likened to all other men, not separated
from them. He is a real man, who entered
into life after the manner common to all the
other children of men, because He must really
belong to ordinary humanity in order to bear
all its carnal and psychical burdens upon the
Cross. For the same reason the apostle adds :
"born under the law," because humanity in its
minority was under the dispensation of the
law ; and forasmuch as in Him humanity was
for the first time to undergo the crisis of
evolution towards a higher life, it behoved
Christ to possess the essential features of the
former period, flesh and the discipline of law.[1]
To maintain that Paul's system logically re-
quires the conception of the supernatural

[1] A. SABATIER, *L'origine du péché dans le système
théologique de Paul*, Paris 1887, p. 36.—*Cf.* REUSS, *Les
Epîtres pauliniennes*, t. I. (1878), p. 114. The formula used
does not express a word more than Job xiv. 1 ; Matt. xi. 11.
Cf. also Rom. v. 15 ; ix. 5 ; 1 Cor. xv. 21 ; 1 Tim. ii. 5.

birth, one must have begun by confusing the Pauline conception of sin and the flesh with the official doctrine of the fall and original sin.[1]

A few other indications contained in several books of the New Testament agree in a most striking manner with the Pauline standpoint. In the speech attributed, in the Acts, to Peter on the day of Pentecost, the apostle, quoting a psalm of David, comments on his text in the following words: "David, being a prophet, knew that God had sworn with an oath to him, that of the fruit of his loins one should sit upon his throne" (Acts ii. 30). The Greek phrases used by the author are faithfully modelled on a Hebraism which expresses with much clearness and force the idea of natural generation.[2] A similar expression is to be found in Paul's speech at Pisidian Antioch, which we read in the

[1] See for example GODET, *Commentaire sur l'épître aux Romains,* i. (1879), pp. 162–163.

[2] Ἐκ καρποῦ τῆς ὀσφύος αὐτοῦ. *Cf.* Ps. cxxxii. 11 : καρπὸς τῆς ὀσφύος αὐτοῦ.

thirteenth chapter of the book of the Acts [1] : "of this man's race (seed) hath God according to promise brought unto Israel a Saviour, Jesus." Anyone who will compare these expressions with the terminology current among the Hebrews and preserved in the Old Testament [2] will soon become convinced that nothing else can here be meant except birth according to the ordinary process of nature.

The Johannine literature [3] is probably later in date than the formation of the dogma of the supernatural birth, witnessed to by the narratives of Matthew and Luke. It might well therefore have embodied the tradition; and yet it has passed it over in silence. Of course

[1] Acts xiii. 23; Ἀπὸ τοῦ σπέρματος . . . *Cf.* 2 Tim. ii. 8 : " Remember Jesus Christ, risen from the dead, of the seed of David. ἐκ σπέρματος Δαυίδ." THRAEN only overcomes the difficulties presented by these expressions, as also by Rom. i. 3, by adopting afresh the harmonizers' old expedient of the Davidic descent of the Virgin Mary, *op. cit.*, 108, 87.

[2] Gen. xxi. 13; xii. 7; xiii. 15, 16; xv. 18; xvii. 8; xxiv. 7; xxvi. 3, 4; xxxv. 12; xv. 5; xix. 32; Deut. xxv. 5–9; 2 Sam. vii. 12; 2 Kings xi. 1.

[3] See Note IX., p. 123.

this silence on the part of the Evangelist in the course of his narrative would not constitute a decisive argument against the miraculous birth. It would not be at all surprising had the latter been unknown at Capernaum or in the neighbourhood [1]; to divulge the secret of this origin " would have been to lay the holiest family mystery open to profane and useless discussion." [2]

But it is more difficult to understand the attitude of the brethren of Jesus ; the Evangelist simply mentions their incredulity,[3] without adding the slightest comment. Finally, we may ask ourselves why the author, when he is giving us his own views and unfolding the content of his faith in Jesus Christ, never refers to the miraculous birth. The only acceptable answer is that the sacred writer " had found in the Logos theory a deeper explanation, and to his mind a better one, of

[1] John vi. 42 ; i. 46. *Cf.* vii. 41.
[2] GODET, *Commentaire sur l'évangile de saint Jean,* ii [2]. (1877), p. 494.
[3] John vii. 5.

the divinity of Christ."[1] The author of the fourth Gospel is here fully in accord with the apostle Paul, who, for his part, had found in the resurrection of the Son of God the key which, in the Johannine theory, was furnished by the doctrine of the Word Incarnate.

I have tried briefly to examine the official doctrine from the exegetical standpoint. Are the conclusions yielded by a study of the Biblical writings favourable to the traditional dogma?[2] Or has historical criticism shaken the scriptural basis on which the clause in the so-called Apostles' Creed rests? I confess that for me the answer to this question does not seem to admit of a doubt. The strainings of exegetes at their wits' end and of harmonizers in despair are not calculated to win confidence and to dispel doubt or uneasiness.

[1] See Note X., p. 123.

[2] On the singularly bold explanation of WEISS (*op. cit.*, i. 257 *sqq.*), who from the very silence of the N. T. writings tries to draw the most decisive proof in favour of the historicity of the supernatural birth, read the excellent remarks of BEYSCHLAG, *op. cit.*, i. 168. *Cf.* HAUPT, *Theologische Studien und Kritiken*, 1884, pp. 57–58.

I need a stronger foundation on which to build my faith in Jesus Christ, and I should feel that were I to rest my belief on so unsafe and threatened a ground, I should never reach a firm and joyful certainty. In making such an avowal there is no danger of my casting a slur upon the dignity or the authority of the Master, who never, even within the circle of His most intimate disciples, made the slightest allusion to this mystery, so true is it that He was able to plant and to ripen, in the hearts of His apostles and in His Church, religious faith in His person, without ever appealing to the miracle of His unique origin!

III

But criticism is not only able to deprive the traditional doctrine of the exegetical support which orthodoxy would fain borrow from our Scriptures. That is only the preliminary and purely negative part of our task. It remains for us to explain positively the historical genesis of the idea of the supernatural birth, to exhibit the true factors which created that conception, to give an account of the elements composing the tradition, which, in the Gospels of Matthew and Luke, has assumed a form so naïvely and touchingly beautiful. This explanation will complete the overthrow of the basis on which the official dogma rests; in addition it will even at this point shew its comparative lawfulness, that is, its religious value.

It is superfluous to prove at any length that what called forth in the hearts of the first disciples their faith in Jesus Christ was the personal experience they gained as they listened to His words and lived in His presence. They felt that the life which the Master lived and which He imparted to them was a divine life; a personal tie of joyful trust and mutual reliance grew up between the Lord and His community; under the influence of the new spirit which proceeded from Him, those who believed in Him gradually modified the carnal and earthly ideal of their traditional Messiah,

in order to harmonize it with the character of
Him who had come to fulfil, not to destroy
the law and the prophets. At first this experience was expressed in the forms consecrated by Israel's religious past and the ardent
preoccupations of contemporary Judaism. By
initiating His disciples into the spiritual depths
of His own religious consciousness, Jesus
elicited the avowal which went up spontane-
ously from their hearts to their lips and which
was expressed with such strong assurance in
the apostle Peter's Messianic confession.
Primitive faith in Jesus Christ necessarily
took the form suggested by Israel's religious
tradition : "Jesus is the Messiah." We know
that the expression *Son of God* was one of
the titles of honour given to the Messiah ; it
is not surprising that, on many occasions, Jesus
should have been called Son of God in the
Messianic sense.[1] As soon as primitive faith

[1] Mark xiv. 61; iii. 11; v. 7; Matt. iv. 3–6; viii. 29;
iii. 17; xvii. 5. The expression "the Son" used by Jesus
is synonymous with the term "Son of God." Matt. xi. 27;
Mark xiii. 32. *Cf.* Matt. xvii. 25–26; xxi. 37; Mark xii. 6.

had recognised and hailed Jesus as the mouth-piece and elect one of God, this religious faith had to identify itself with belief in the Messiah. We may hardly yet speak of a dogmatic explanation, so direct and spontaneous is the feeling asserted in Peter's words: " Thou art the Christ of God." Still, considering that from the very beginning reflection seized upon the data of faith and translated into beliefs the original affirmations of sentiment, it is not inaccurate to say that the oldest notion of the divine sonship of Jesus was *theocratic.*

Is it necessary to prove that this primitive conception could very well subsist side by side with the idea of the natural birth of the Messiah? The error of the older theology, which invested the first disciples with a clear perception of all the later developments of Christian dogmas, is now all but unanimously condemned by modern orthodoxy.[1] The

[1] It is true that HENGSTENBERG, for example, still adheres to the old orthodox position. Orthodox theology now-

primitive, theocratic and Messianic faith in Jesus in no way implied a settled opinion as to the manner of Christ's entrance into the world. The immediate followers of Jesus, not only the crowd that pressed around Him, but also the inner circle of His disciples, undoubtedly looked upon Jesus of Nazareth as the son of Joseph and Mary.[1]

But religious faith in the Messiahship of Jesus soon developed the consequences latent within itself, and these consequences, owing to the pressure of various circumstances, were gradually evolved out of the primitive germ and expressed in theological formulas. Dogmatic thought, trying to interpret the fact given by historical revelation and inward experience, did not rest content with defining the impression produced by Christ, it also endeavoured to explain the nature and origin of the Lord's personality. Still concerned for the religious wel-

adays has a saner conception of historical conditions and development. (See GODET, *Comment. on St. Luke,* i. 158.)

[1] Matt. xiii. 55; Mark vi. 3; Luke iv. 22; John i. 46; vi. 42. See also Note XI., p. 124.

fare of the Faith, Christian theology sought this explanation in the Messianic interpretation of the Old Testament, and in Rabbinical or Alexandrine speculation. The dominant speculation which inspired exegesis seems at first to have seized hold of the notion of the pre-existence of Christ. In fact, the oldest Christological documents contained in the New Testament teach the personal pre-existence of the Son of God. Paul's idea of this divine existence of Christ, prior to His manifestation on earth, may be a matter for discussion; but it cannot be doubted that in the mind of the apostle the Lord's personality has a heavenly and spiritual origin.

In formulating this speculative thesis, the apostle was only applying to Christ one of the most important philosophical and religious categories of his day: he was expressing, in the theological language current in the schools, the divine worth which his faith put upon the Lord's work and person. Later Pauline developments, combined with Alexandrian tendencies, carried on the tradition inaugurated by the apostles and followed by the Christian editor of the Apocalypse. Finally, the Johannine gnosis appropriated the conception of the Logos, worked it into the Gospel story, identified it with the person of Christ, and found in the theory of the Word Incarnate the key to the destinies of humanity and the secret of the creation itself.[1] The primitive conception, which is apparent in the few Christological indications of the book of Acts, and is at the root of the Synoptic narrative, was thus left behind by the dogmatic development of the Christian consciousness. The notion of the divine sonship of Jesus was drawn into the stream of this theological evolution, and was subjected to a change consonant with the particular point of view of the speculation. To the purely theocratic conception of the divine filiation of the Messiah was added, if not substituted for it, the *metaphysical* explanation.

[1] See Note XII., p. 124.

The canonical writings which embody this theological interpretation of the person and work of Christ nowhere mention, as we have already seen, the fact of the miraculous birth of Jesus. It is the precise fact that the speculative and metaphysical solution was an attempt to give an account of the nature and origin of the Son of God. The writers who had found in this explanation their answer to the Christological problem did not feel the need of seeking any subsidiary solution. Did either of them know of the narratives of Matthew and Luke? In all probability, yet they made no use of them and they nowhere refer to them. They are not considering the person and work of Jesus from the point of view of Christ according to the flesh, but in the light of the glorified Lord or of the Logos who is one with the Father.

Between the primitive outlook of popular Messianic belief and the point reached by speculative thought in the prologue to the fourth Gospel, we may place the tradition

5

which has been preserved in the double narrative of the Protevangel.[1] Matthew and Luke make known to us a third form, in which the divine sonship of Christ found expression during the second generation of Christians, a form indicative of further thought, and more theological than the Messianic declaration, more concrete and realistic than the metaphysical solution : the explanation disclosed in the Gospels of the nativity is the *physical* explanation of the divine sonship of Jesus.

Such is the original meaning, such the primitive bearing of the religious and theological idea which has taken shape in the story of the supernatural conception and of the miraculous birth of Jesus.   Let us try to shew this.

The scene of the Annunciation, related by Luke, contains a conclusive indication on this point ; we have, from the mouth of the angel himself, the authentic explanation of the term *Son of God*.[2] " The Holy Ghost shall come

[1] See Note XIII., p. 126.   [2] GODET, *op. cit.,* i. 93.

upon thee, and the power of the Most High shall overshadow thee : therefore also the holy child shall be called the Son of God." [1] The logical connection of the sentence would be broken if the divine sonship of Jesus did not rest, according to the angel's declaration, upon the miraculous conception of the holy child in the virgin's womb. The expression Son of God must here be taken in its most literal sense; the Holy Ghost is the author of the corporeal and material life of Jesus, the maker of His whole personality : the divine sonship of Christ implies a communication of the substance of God, it is a *physical* filiation.[2]

A more minute study of this notion of the divine sonship will make us understand the scope of this affirmation, and will show us that it is the concrete and material representation of a highly religious idea.

It is well known that the religious genius of

---

[1] Luke i. 35. Best supported reading : διὸ καὶ τὸ γεννώμενον ἅγιον κληθήσεται υἱὸς θεοῦ, Sanctum illud procreatum ; *cf.* Matt. i. 20 : τὸ γὰρ ἐν αὐτῇ γεννηθέν.

[2] See Note XIV., p. 126.

Israel, as indeed the religious sense in general, is essentially characterized by its suppression of all secondary causes and its demonstration of the direct action of the will of God in all things. The historians of the theocracy, bent on pointing out divine intervention in the history of the chosen people, frequently try to discover at the outset of the life of the national and religious heroes extraordinary signs of providential intervention. But the editors of the historical books of the Old Testament were merely the interpreters of the popular faith. This faith, taking a poetic form in myths, often penetrated with deep or naïve religious inspiration, hailed the appearance of its liberators and prophets as a manifestation of deliverance on the part of Jahweh or as the realization of some divine purpose. The birth of these chosen instruments of the Eternal could be nothing short of the result of a sovereign and merciful act of the God of Israel. The poetic traditions which surround the cradles of Isaac, Samson and Samuel are the outcome of this religious instinct, which spoke by turns the language of pastoral poetry, of warlike epic, or of prophetic lyricism.[1]

From the religion of Israel this religious conception passed into the consciousness of early Christianity and inspired the piety of the men of the new covenant. In the celebrated allegory of Hagar the apostle Paul contrasts the child born after the order of nature with the child born after the spirit. Ishmael, the son of the bondwoman, is the child κατὰ σάρκα, according to the flesh. The birth of Isaac is represented as miraculous, not because the mode of his birth was exceptional (Isaac is indeed the son of Abraham and Sarah), but because a divine factor, "a word of promise," had intervened in the natural course of events and had enabled Abraham to become, in spite of Sarah's already advanced age, the father of Isaac and of a numerous posterity : Isaac is the child of promise, the son promised by the sovereign power and gracious faithfulness of the Eternal

---

[1] Gen. xv., xvii., xviii., xxi. ; Judges xiii. ; 1 Sam. i.

in answer to the faith and obedience of
Abraham. The apostle does not deny the
secondary causes and the human factors to
which Isaac owed his birth, but he passes them
over, that he may take into account nothing
but the immediate will of God. What matters,
is not his natural descent, but his spiritual
sonship, as a prophetic type of the birth of
believers.[1]

The Gospel of Luke contains a story which
presents a striking parallel with the history of
the birth of Isaac. John the Baptist, the son
of Zacharias and Elizabeth, is, like Isaac, the
subject of persistent prayer answered, as in the
case of Sarah, at a time when the answer
seemed impossible of fulfilment. John, the
child of promise, like the son of Abraham and
Sarah, receives a measure of grace, of which the

[1] Gal. iv. 29; Ὁ κατὰ σάρκα γεννηθείς . . . τὸν κατὰ
πνεῦμα . . . cf. v. 28; ὑμεῖς δὲ, ἀδελφοί, κατὰ Ἰσαὰκ
ἐπαγγελίας τέκνα ἐστέ.—Cf. Rom. ix. 8; οὐ τὰ τέκνα τῆς
σαρκὸς ταῦτα τέκνα τοῦ θεοῦ, ἀλλὰ τὰ τέκνα τῆς ἐπαγγελίας.
THRAEN's contention (112–113) rests upon a misconception
gratuitously ascribed to the author.

older tradition makes no mention, he is filled
with the Holy Ghost even from his mother's
womb[1] (Luke i. 7, 13, 15, 44).

Have we not here a notion very much akin
to that which lies behind the narratives of the
miraculous birth of Jesus? If the faith of
Israel invested the ancestors and heroes of the
nation with a privilege which at the outset set
a divine seal upon them, is it surprising that the
Christian consciousness, absolutely convinced
of the divine nature of the work and inspiration
of Christ, should have attempted to explain the
birth and nature of the Messiah by a greater
miracle than any which had presided over the
origin of the most famous prophets? Being
greater than those who *received* the Holy
Spirit from their earliest infancy, He was *conceived* by the Holy Spirit[2]; His life proceeds
directly from the life of God himself; His
entire personality is an immediate creation of

[1] See Note XV., p. 127.
[2] A. RÉVILLE, *op. cit.*, p. 29. *Cf.* BEYSCHLAG, *Leben Jesu*,
i. 162.

the divine activity ; the primitive and essential relationship which unites Jesus to God is not only a bond of spiritual sonship, it embraces the life of the body no less than that of the soul : the divine sonship of Jesus is a physical filiation.

Thus understood, the fact of the miraculous birth of Christ is only the material expression of an experience of the Christian consciousness, brought into contact with the person and work of Jesus. From the divine character of this work and person, it concludes that they are both divine in origin ; like the speculative thesis of the pre-existence of Christ, the Gospel narrative of the supernatural birth of Jesus is an explanatory formula, an attempt to solve the Christological problem ; if the theory of the pre-existence is the theological corollary of a religious axiom, the story of the miraculous birth is not so much the result of dogmatic thought as the fruit of popular imagination.[1]

[1] *Cf.* the remarks of KAFTAN, *Das Wesen der christlichen Religion.* Basel ; 1881, pp. 315–316.

This work of poetical and religious creation, prompted by faith, was carried forward by the methods of interpretation current during early Christian times. The new faith, in quest of arguments and illustrations furnished by the Old Testament, hit upon a prophetic passage which provided religious feeling with its exact and definite formula. We mean, of course, the famous verse in Isaiah vii. 14 quoted by Matthew from the Septuagint. " Now all this is come to pass, says the Evangelist, that it might be fulfilled which was spoken by the Lord through the prophet, saying: Behold, the virgin shall be with child, and shall bring forth a son, and they shall call his name Immanuel; which is, being interpreted, God with us " (Matt. i. 22–23). The context of the prophetic utterance clearly shews its meaning and bearing. King Ahaz, threatened by the kings of Syria and Israel, is urged by the prophet to ask for a sign, by which he may see that Isaiah is not deceiving him, when he reassures him as to the issue of the war.

The sign, which Ahaz refuses, is given by
the prophet, who nevertheless, in order to
punish the king for his distrust, adds after the
promise of safety a dark and terrible prospect
for the future. The proffered sign foretells
safety. "The Lord himself shall give you a
sign ; behold a virgin shall conceive and bear a
son, and shall call his name ' God with us.'"
The Hebrew term denotes a young woman,
neither Isaiah's wife nor any other woman in
particular, but any woman living in the
prophet's time. When a woman is with child
the date of her delivery may be calculated.
And so Isaiah proclaims that a happy change will
shortly take place, even within a few months,
circumstances will have become so reassuring,
that, under the influence of victory and success,
the mother will call her new-born babe " God
with us " ! Such is the meaning of this
passage, the Messianic interpretation of which
belongs not to the original Hebrew, but to
the Alexandrian Version. The translators rendered the word הָעַלְמָה which cannot mean

virgin (compare Cant. vi. 8 *sq.*, and especially
Prov. xxx. 19 *sq.*) by ἡ παρθένος[1]; thus
they paved the way for the religious construc-
tion adopted by the Evangelist.[2]

It is therefore unnecessary to resort to the
hypothesis of pagan influences or of Hellenic
or Oriental factors in order to explain the
origin of the belief in the supernatural birth of
Christ. The tradition consecrated by our
Gospels, the myth[3] with which faith in the
divine sonship of Jesus is poetically invested,
has its roots deep down in Israel's religion,
transformed by the new faith. The dogma of
the supernatural birth is the result of the union
of traditional interpretation with the Christian
principle. Recent researches,[4] completing and

---

[1] The word בְּתוּלָה, which means Virgin, is used more
than fifty times in the Old Testament; it is the term which
would have been used by the prophet to express the idea
attributed to him by the LXX.

[2] See REUSS, *Les prophètes*, t. i. (1876), pp. 233–234.
The author's judicious remark is unanswerable: "Wha
consolation would Ahaz have had, if the prophet had said
to him: Do not fear these two kings, in seven hundred
and fifty years the Messiah will be born?"

[3] See Note XVI., p. 127.   [4] See Note XVII., p. 128.

enriching observations made long ago, have collected numerous and often striking analogies between the Biblical myth and legends of Greek or Eastern origin. Yet in such analogies it would be rash to see direct imitations or positive influences. The aversion which primitive Christianity felt for polytheistic paganism was so deep-seated that before supposing the new religion to have been influenced by pagan mythologies, we must examine with the utmost possible care the points of resemblance which are sometimes found to exist between beliefs and institutions. No doubt the history of the Church abundantly proves that between the worship or doctrine of paganism on the one hand and advancing Christianity on the other, there was mutual action and, so to speak, slow and constant infiltration, but nothing warrants historical criticism in considering the tradition of the miraculous birth of Christ as merely the outcome of elements foreign to the religion of Biblical revelation.[1]

[1] See Note XVIII., p. 130.

Thus analysed into its primitive elements and explained in its inner genesis, the dogma or myth inspired by religious faith, created by popular imagination, sanctioned by the hermeneutics of the School, takes its place in the historical development of the dogma of the person of Christ.[1] It represents one of the stages in the doctrinal evolution which, starting with the theocratic conception of primitive Messianic expectation, rose to the speculative notion of the metaphysical pre-existence of the Messiah. It is impossible to fix the date of the full blossoming of "the pastoral epic of Christianity"[2]; the notion of the miraculous birth is one of its integral and prominent features. Even if the documents which teach the metaphysical pre-existence of Christ are older than those which explain the divine sonship of Jesus by a physical miracle, it is by

[1] Cf. KEIM, History of Jesus of Nazara, vol. ii., p. 59 sqq. ; BIEDERMANN, Christliche Dogmatik, §§ 241, 242, 249, 263, 582 ; REUSS, op. cit., pp. 139-140 ; STRAUSS, Die christliche Glaubenslehre, ii. 85–87.

[2] A. SABATIER, Encyclopédie des sciences religieuses, vii. 379.

no means proved that the origin of the latter solution is subsequent to the elaboration of the theory of the pre-existence, for Matthew and Luke only received and set down in writing far older traditions.

Have I succeeded in explaining the origin of the dogma of the supernatural birth contained in the mythical narrative of our first and third Gospels? Were the reader to deem that the explanation offered does not remove the difficulties, and that our positive criticism of the dogma does not solve the problem, still the negative results yielded by exegesis would none the less remain entire. What then remains of the objection which faced us at the beginning of our inquiry? Is it true that, in order successfully to defend the official doctrine, it is enough to appeal to Biblical testimony? Are traditional Apologetics happily inspired or acting wisely, in confining the debate within the limits of exegesis and history? Theology has evidently looked upon this series of arguments as inadequate, seeing that it has not been content to appeal to Scripture texts in support of the dogma of the supernatural conception of Christ. Or rather, the arguments drawn from exegesis are themselves inspired by dogmatic prepossessions and religious interests easily discoverable. In a word, those theologians who had recalled us to the letter of our Gospels and whom we had followed into the region of exegesis and criticism, give us to understand or openly aver that at the back of this discussion of texts and of this analysis of documents there is a graver and deeper question. What must finally turn the scale, I mean determine belief and carry conviction, are reasons of a dogmatic and religious order, which find their high authority in our Gospels, and, in turn, give them their complete and final justification. The official doctrine must be studied from the point of view of dogma and religion.

IV

The opinion, most generally accredited in the ranks of popular orthodoxy, is that the miraculous birth is a necessary condition of the Saviour's sinlessness. This opinion has been promoted and defended by means of numerous and varied arguments; but the common idea at the root of all essays in Apologetics is the Augustinian theory of a fall of the human race, of an hereditary taint handed down by natural generation; that Christ might be free from the original taint imparted to the human race by Adam's transgression, it behoved Him to be conceived by the Holy Ghost and born of a Virgin. "The absolute purity of this birth results, on the one hand, from the perfect holiness of the divine principle which is its efficient cause; on the other, from the absence of every impure motion in her who becomes a mother under the power of such a principle." [1]

This first attempt at explanation and dog-

---

[1] GODET, *op. cit.*, i. 93. *Cf.* THOMASIUS, *Christi Person und Werk*, ii. (1857), p. 130 *et seq.* KRAUSS, *Die Lehre von der Offenbarung*, Ein Beitrag zur Philosophie des Christenthums. Gotha 1868, pp. 322–323. THRAEN, *op. cit.*, 121–135; SANDAY, *art. cit.*, p. 69.

matic justification does not bear serious and impartial examination.

In the first place it finds no support in our texts; neither Matthew nor Luke warrant our accepting such an explanation. Read again attentively the narratives of our two Evangelists; weigh carefully the meaning of the context of Luke i. 35, and you will certainly have to admit that the orthodox explanation can only be maintained by the help of considerations and proofs primitively foreign to our Gospel records. The Holy Spirit spoken of in Matthew (i. 20) and Luke (i. 35) is the divine virtue, the life-giving breath, the creative force, which is the attribute of the omnipotence of God. The Old Testament gives us the key to this expression, familiar among the Israelites[1]; the ethical and religious conception of purity and of the freedom from all taint is not implied

---

[1] *Cf.* Kleinert, *Zur alttestamentlichen Lehre von Geiste Gottes* (Jahrbücher für deutsche Theologie, 1867, p. 1 *et seq.*) A. Sabatier, *Encyclopédie des sciences religieuses*, t. iv. p. 540 *et seq.*; *id.*, *Mémoire sur la notion hébraïque de l'Esprit*, 1879.

in the term πνεῦμα ἅγιον, which, in our writings, does not bear the theological and dogmatic complexion given to it by the apostle Paul.[1] The manifest parallelism which exists between the words πνεῦμα ἅγιον and δύναμις ὑψίστου would alone be sufficient to dispel all uncertainty (Luke i. 35).

In the second place, we must recall that no passage in the New Testament establishes the slightest connection between the miraculous birth of Jesus and His perfect sinlessness. Our Gospels and Paul nowhere account for the moral and religious purity of " Him who knew no sin " (2 Cor. v. 21), by the fact of the immaculate conception of Christ in Mary's womb. Neither is the more timid explanation, put forth by an orthodoxy less staunch than was our fathers', better countenanced by the Scriptures ; for where, pray, is it stated that the miraculous birth was the *negative* condition of the immaculate holiness of Jesus ? How can it be exegetically maintained that " enter-

[1] See Note XIX., p. 131.

ing into human life in this way, He was
placed in the normal condition of man before
his fall, and put in a position to fulfil the
career originally set before man, in which
he was to advance from innocence to holiness " ? [1] Without doubt it is right that
we should gratefully acknowledge the motive
which prompts modern orthodoxy to mitigate
the uncompromising rigour of old formulas ; it
is desired to safeguard the moral reality of the
life of Jesus, to exhibit His holiness as a result
of will, not of nature ; but it is impossible for
this mitigated and more rational conception
to appeal to the witness of any Biblical
text.

Besides, this view starts from faulty premises.
It takes for granted that our Evangelists knew
and approved of the Augustinian doctrine of
the original and hereditary sin of the human
race ; now, this theory elaborated by Augustine
under the influence of preoccupations very far

[1] GODET, *op. cit.,* i. 94. *Cf.* GODET, *Biblical Studies, New
Test.,* pp. 90–91.

removed from exegesis, is totally absent from our Synoptic Gospels. The apostle Paul himself did not hold it in the sense put upon it by the celebrated father of the Church.[1] If it is true that the traditional idea of the birth of Jesus, without the intervention of a human father, was strengthened by the official doctrine of the fall, it is nevertheless contrary both to the letter and the spirit of our Gospel sources to maintain that Luke and Matthew looked upon the story of the miraculous conception as a proof that Jesus was free from the taint of original sin.

Irreconcilable with the positive and unanimous witness of our Biblical documents, this attempt to found the sinlessness of Christ on the miracle of His birth is in itself altogether illusory and unfortunate. The difficulty which the traditional explanation raises and the insoluble contradiction which it contains have

[1] A. SABATIER, *L'origine du péché dans le système théologique de Paul.* Paris, 1887, p. 6 *et seq.* HOLTZMANN, *Lehrbuch der neutestamentlichen Theologie,* ii. 44.

often been pointed out.[1] Does the exclusion of the human father answer to the postulate which it is intended to safeguard? Does not the transmission of sin take place through the mother as well as through the father?[2] Was not Mary's flesh, too, stained by original sin? Does not the traditional conception necessarily lead either to Docetism, according to which Christ was not born of (ἐκ) Mary, but through (διά) her who was His reputed mother,[3] or to the Roman doctrine which extends the immaculate conception from Jesus to Mary and passes on the state of sinlessness from Him to her?[4] But this is not all: must we not go

---

[1] *Cf.* Schleiermacher, *Der Christliche Glaube*, § 97. Strauss, *Das Leben Jesu, kritisch bearbeitet*, i. (1835), pp. 153–154. Rückert, *Theologie*, ii. (1851), 137. Calvin had already felt the inadequacy of this argumentation. *Inst.*, ii. 13, 4.

[2] See Note XX., p. 131.

[3] Such was the opinion of certain Gnostics, Valentinus, for example. *Cf.* Tertullian, *Adv. Valent.*, xxvii.

[4] The excellent article by A. Réville in *L'Encyclopédie des sciences religieuses* (iii. 288–291) gives a summary account of the principal stages in the evolution of Catholic dogma.

back along the line of ancestry until we arrive at Eve herself, and postulate an uninterrupted chain of miracles appointed to preserve from spot of sin that progeny which, extending over centuries, was finally to lead up to Mary and Jesus ? To forestall the absurd consequences which logically flow from the premises of the official doctrine, contemporary orthodoxy has not shrunk from imitating the Scholastic theologians of the Middle Ages and from bringing physiology into dogma.[1] We are assured that in order to secure the negative condition of the perfect holiness of Jesus, the elimination of the paternal factor is amply sufficient. It is true that the most accredited representatives of this physiological dogmatism are not fully agreed[2]; but they are at one in asserting that the suppression of natural generation implies the absence of every impure motion and constitutes an absolutely effective preservative

[1] See, *e.g.*, ANSELM, *Cur Deus homo,* ii. 8. HARNACK, *History of Dogma,* iii. 276.

[2] See Note XXI., p. 132.

against all moral contamination: as if the objective principle in original sin was not, in the light of the consecrated dogma sanely understood, essentially immanent in the flesh of Mary, outside the particular moment of conception! as if the natural laws which, in obedience to the will of the Creator, preside over the propagation of the human race were irremediably tainted with sin and sullied by impurity! as if the new spiritual creation which came in with Jesus Christ could only have been realized at the price of a slur cast upon the essential conditions of physical and natural creation![1]

But let us abandon a discussion which wanders in regions whither we are loath to follow dogmatists who know not when to ignore. Nevertheless we may perhaps be allowed to give expression in all sincerity to an opinion which we are unable to resist: we pity a theology which finds itself compelled to seek in the mysterious functions of the physical

[1] See below, § V.

organism the final explanation of a religious dogma and one of the foundations of our Christian faith.[1]

Yet the miraculous birth of Christ is not only looked upon as the positive or negative condition of the perfect sinlessness of the Saviour; official theology also considers this dogma as the necessary basis of the fact of the Incarnation. "The miraculous birth is inseparable from the fact of the Incarnation," i.e., the idea of natural birth is incompatible with the Incarnation. The traditional doctrine combines the notion of the eternal and essential pre-existence of the Word with the idea of the miraculous birth. "From the pre-existence follows the necessity of an exceptional mode of birth."[2] If it is true that Jesus Christ is the Word made flesh, it is necessary that having been eternally begotten of the substance of the Father, He should have been, in

[1] See Note XXII., p. 132.
[2] GODET, *op. cit.*, i. 160. *Cf.* PHILIPPI, *Kirchliche Glaubenslehre*, iv. 1 (1861), 144. WENNAGEL, *op. cit.*, p. 58.

order to become a member of humanity, conceived by the Holy Ghost and born of a virgin. Such is the declaration of official theology in all Christian confessions.

It is easy to see that this declaration combines two conceptions, essentially different and primitively quite independent. On the one hand, the first and third Gospels wholly ignore the notion of the pre-existence of the Word; nor do they contain the slightest trace of this metaphysical explanation of the divinity of Christ; on the other, the writers who mention or teach the pre-existence of the Logos nowhere make even the faintest reference to the tradition of the miraculous birth. The historical origin of both theories is radically different, and to combine them or to explain the one by the other is to do violence to our texts. It is also to distort the peculiar and distinctive character of each of these two doctrines. It is perfectly certain that Matthew and Luke, when describing the manner of the entrance of Jesus into the world, exhibit a conception totally different from that implied by Pauline or Johannine theology. They are speaking of the birth of a being who does not yet exist and who owes his birth to the supernatural action of the divine Spirit "coming upon Mary"; the conception of a self pre-existing throughout all eternity and taking in the womb of the virgin either human nature in addition to the divine[1] or another form of existence following on the divine existence,[2] such a conception has absolutely nothing in common with the more popular tradition of our first and third Gospels.[3] What would therefore remain to be examined would be the value and basis of the speculative and metaphysical theory of the pre-existing Logos. Such a study naturally lies outside the range of the present essay.[4]

A last attempt to prove the religious and dogmatic necessity for the supernatural birth

[1] Orthodox theory of the official Church.
[2] Heterodox theory of the modern Kenosis.
[3] See Note XXIII., p. 133.   [4] See above, § III.

of Christ deserves to engage our attention; the attempt is specially interesting in view of the fact that some of the theologians who initiated it appear in some degree prepared to sacrifice the notion of the eternal and personal pre-existence of the Word. They wish to substitute for this dogmatic thesis, the historical explanation furnished by the fact of the miraculous birth of Christ. The Saviour, they tell us, was the second Adam, the head of a new humanity, the type of man answering to the eternal purpose of God; we must, therefore, be able to find in Him every perfection to which human nature is capable of attaining; He cannot have possessed a distinctive character or a particular individuality, because He gathered up in Himself all individualities and characters; the Son of God is a "central personality," a collective being who sums up and raises to their highest expression the special capacities of all individual units. He cannot, therefore, have been the son of any particular man: originator of a new humanity, He must needs be the son of humanity, the son of man, created in the bosom of natural humanity by a sovereign act of God's supernatural power. The narratives of the miraculous birth alone satisfy this religious and dogmatic postulate.[1]

It seems to me enough to set forth and describe this theory in order to pronounce its absolute and irrevocable condemnation. It is easy to draw up the certificate of birth of this explanation which once successfully held the field. The famous Christological solution by means of the " central personality " dates back from a time and a school which substituted speculation for history and the uncertain dreams of the imagination for the positive realities of life. The human ideal which a few German thinkers imagined they dimly perceived from the lofty and cloud-capped summits of their so-called Christian metaphysics is a pure abstraction. Hear M. Sabatier: " In order to have every distinctive

[1] See Note XXIV., p. 134.

mark, Jesus must possess none. It must not be asked whether He offered the type of the artist, of the scientist, of the statesman, or of the man engaged in any particular avocation. He was not great in every department. For Him, human life in its manifoldness was entirely under the rule of religion and ethics. It is there, in the realm of holiness, of the keeping of the law, of the attainment of imperative ideals, in this general and purely human realm, anterior to every specialization, but found in each, it is there that Jesus has set the example, that is where He remains the perfect model. For in Him man on the one hand attains to his full moral stature, and on the other is fully at one with God. After that, it is quite legitimate to speak of an individual character and even of a temperament in Jesus. His personality, far from being in any way vague or indeterminate, was most marked and strong. If it is difficult to depict, it is on account of the happy way in which the apparently contrary forces which constitute it are blended

together."[1] Such is the real and living
personality of the Jesus of our Gospels.
What then becomes of the speculative justification for the dogma of the miraculous birth
of Christ? It vanishes with the Christological
phantom which it was designed to uphold
and which fades away in the clear light of the
Christian revelation.

Thus the principal dogmatic arguments
which have been severally tried to bolster up
the official doctrine formulated in the creed:
*conceptus de spiritu sancto, natus ex Maria
Virgine*, fall to the ground. The dogmatic
basis, which current orthodoxy has attempted
to give to the tradition of the miraculous conception and to the supernatural birth of Christ,
is no sounder than the exegetical and historical
foundation on which the official doctrine rests.[2]

[1] A. SABATIER, *Encyclopédie des sciences religieuses*, vii.
368. *Cf.* HAUPT's excellent remarks (*Theologische Studien
und Kritiken*, 1884, i. 43–45; 1887, ii. 374–377). LIPSIUS,
Lehrbuch der evangelisch-protestantischen Dogmatik, 1876,
§ 650.

[2] See Note XXV., p. 135.

Do we thereby mean that the tradition or myth of the supernatural origin of Jesus of Nazareth is divested of all religious interest and that it does not answer to a postulate of the Christian consciousness? Because the narratives of the Nativity are not real in the literal sense of the word, do they lose their religious value and their truth? Does poetry, by taking the place of history, cease to be the inspired messenger of a divine thought? Surely not, if it be true that "the Spirit of God may be present in poetry as well, and sometimes better, than in history."[1] Let us try to unravel the Christian principle which lies hidden behind the transparent veil of the Gospel symbolism.

V

In order to reduce the official doctrine to its purely religious import, we need only to resolve the Gospel tradition into its primitive

[1] A. SABATIER, *Encyclopédie des sciences religieuses,* vii. 378–379.

elements and the factors which built it up.

Our research into the genesis of the myth of the "nativity" has proved to us that the conception of the miraculous birth of Christ is the fruit of religious feeling, the echo of Christian experience, the poetic and popular expression of an affirmation of faith. The important thing for us is to defend this affirmation, to safeguard this experience in all its force and purity.

What is the object of the religious affirmation of faith, the living centre and essence of the Christian experience?

By his faith in Jesus Christ, by his personal experience when he enters into communion with the Saviour, the Christian feels that the life imparted by his Lord is a divine life. In Christ, in His person and work, he is certain that he has found God, a God of love and mercifulness. The faith of the Christian fully assents to the saying of Christ: "He that hath seen me hath seen the Father."[1] Yes,

[1] John xiv. 9.

henceforth we know that the love of God, whom we are allowed to call our Father, is not an empty wish, a vague promise or a fine theory; this love is even now an actual gift, this love is a reality, a power and a life. The infinite mercy of God which wills not the death of a sinner, that eternal charity for which our heart yearns and in which alone it finds pardon and peace, the charity of God has appeared in humanity, has lived upon this earth, has been made flesh; it has a name in history, we can gaze upon it, hear it, see it with our eyes and handle it with our hands.[1] Jesus Christ has shewn us the Father, He has revealed Him to us in His own person, for He loved us as God himself loved the world. Yea, more: through the radiancy of this love which has filled my life and illumined its darkest depths, I confidently believe that redeeming grace is no far-distant story belonging to a past which has for ever vanished away; I confidently believe and proclaim that the infinite love, which created

[1] John i. 14–18; 1 John i. 1–3.

7

the world, and presides over the destinies of history, has reached down even to me, has rescued me from the shipwreck in which I was about to sink for ever, has caught and now upholds me in its embrace, and, placing me under the mild and powerful rule of its holy law, inspires me with the desire and gives me the strength to fulfil it! Such is the message which Jesus came to bring to sinning and unhappy souls, a message which was incarnate in His person, and which He pressed home to the centre of our history, to the very heart of our lives. The witness which we bear to our Lord can be none other than the response to what He has done for us and what He now is to us. We care not if, after that, men dispute our right to speak of the divinity of Christ: we will not quarrel over words! But what we know, is that we fully retain, I say fully, the religious content, and therefore the only essential part of what current orthodoxy calls the divinity of Christ, reduced to its simplest expression—to its truly evangelical expression.

The divinity of Jesus Christ! How often has this blessed affirmation of the Christian consciousness been misunderstood! How disfigured it has become, by being turned into I know not what abstract speculation, problem of transcendental metaphysics or unintelligible formula, sometimes so foreign to piety, that simple and naïve faith, in the presence of these difficult and insoluble questions, would cry out in despair: "They have taken away my Lord and I know not where they have laid him!" Confession of the divinity of Christ has no meaning or value except as the spontaneous avowal of a conscience quickened by the Saviour's pity and feeling itself transformed by His spirit.[1] "Lord, to whom shall we go? Thou hast the words of eternal life. And we have believed and know that thou art the Holy One of God."[2] To confess the divinity of Christ is to affirm and to feel personally that He has brought to those who give themselves to Him the peace of a con-

[1] 1 Cor. xii. 3. [2] John vi. 68-69.

science reconciled to God and the power of an endless life; that He has imparted to those who are His a principle of boundless love, of enduring truth, of perfect holiness; that He has substituted for all motives of action drawn from the world and prompted by base reasons, the inspiration of a life issuing from God and actuated by lofty considerations; that to enter into communion with Him is to be united to God himself; that the supreme felicity and inalienable bliss of His disciple is to be one with Him even as He is one with the Father.[1]

If such is the expression of our faith, that is to say the affirmation of our experience, it is perfectly clear that the divine life, incarnate in Jesus Christ and imparted by Him to humanity, proceeds from a divine source, that it did not issue from the low depths of our sin-polluted earth, but that it is the emanation of a force, the ultimate cause and secret of

[1] Such is the religious substance of the farewell speeches of the Johannine Christ. See the theological analysis which I have tried to give of them in *La notion de la préexistence du Fils de Dieu*, 1883, pp. 68–70.

which we do not discover in ourselves. The
personality of Him who was, and who remains
for us the revelation and channel of the divine
love, the personality of the Son of God stands
out to the eye of faith as a new creation, as
the head of a humanity which "has its roots
in heaven," as the second Adam born of
God and living in God.[1] That is the urgent
demand of the Christian faith, which needs to
trace back to the sovereign and all-powerful
grace of the heavenly Father the gift He has
bestowed upon us in the person of His only
Son. If it is true that in Jesus Christ the
divine intention which presided at the creation
was realized, if He is the elect one of God who
was to give to natural and sinful humanity
what in itself it did not possess, we must
conclude that the appearance of the initiator
and dispenser of this divine life necessarily
implies and presupposes a special manifestation
of God, a creative and sanctifying intervention

[1] Cf. ALBARIC, De la personne de Jésus-Christ (Nouvelle
Revue de Théologie, t. ix., Strasbourg, 1862, p. 335 et seq.).

of His Spirit. Such is the affirmation of the Christian consciousness, and our faith could not surrender it without renouncing itself and consummating its own ruin and suicide: such is also the element of truth which the traditional theory contains.[1]

But now we come to the exact point where we must part company with the traditional theory: how did this imparting of divine life to humanity take place? What were the physiological and psychological conditions of the entrance of the Son of God into the world? This question is not identical with the religious postulate formulated by faith; the Christian consciousness is not qualified to settle a problem which is not within its province, but which belongs to the domain of the natural sciences and of historical criticism. The religious interest of the Christian faith does not centre round the mode of origin of Jesus, but in the divine character of His manifestation on earth. What matters is not a belief in the miraculous

[1] See Note XXVI., p. 136.

birth without the co-operation of an earthly
father, but faith in the working of divine grace,
which, in the very heart of humanity itself,
has created a new personality, thus breaking
asunder the chain of sin and inaugurating the
Kingdom of Heaven upon earth.[1]

Is it rash to esteem that such a faith is compromised and dimmed rather than safeguarded
and justified by the official doctrine? I think
not: I even go so far as to believe that there is
no little danger in raising the tradition of the
miraculous birth of Christ to the rank of a
dogma and an article of faith. The method
or the claim of those theologians who make
this tradition the basis or the starting-point of
Christology presents grave drawbacks, and it
is in the name of faith itself that we must rise
up against this summary identification of the
orthodox formula with the religious postulate
of the Christian consciousness.[2]

[1] *Cf.* the remarks of HAUPT, *Theologische Studien und
Kritiken,* 1884, pp. 58–59.
[2] See SCHULTZ, *op. cit.,* pp. 393–394.

It has been proved above that the "Gospel of the infancy of Jesus" formed no part of the early preaching of the Gospel. The personal witness of the Apostles did not bear upon the facts which happened prior to their call to be Apostles. The narratives collected by Matthew and Luke cannot be looked upon as elements forming a part of the Gospel revelation. The defenders of the official doctrine are themselves forced to admit that neither the Master nor His disciples ever appealed to the miraculous conception of Jesus to arouse faith in the Saviour.[1] The Christian faith of those who first saw Jesus was elicited by their close touch with the person and work of Christ; the Apostles believed with their whole hearts in the Saviour, under the inspiration of His spirit, on the ground of His witness, deeds and life; when hailing the Messianic glory of the Son of God, veiled beneath the lowly form of the Son of man, Peter was apparently

[1] *Cf.* for example GODET, *op. cit.*, i. 158. THRAEN, pp. 145–146.

expressing no judgment as to the mode of this sonship, yet he nevertheless received from the Lord's lips the following conclusive declaration, utterance of joyful surprise and sovereign approval: "Blessed art thou, Simon, son of Jonah: for flesh and blood hath not revealed it unto thee, but my Father which is in heaven" (Matt. xvi. 17). Such is, indeed, the living centre of the Gospel revelation, such is the essential object of the Christian faith. The character of revelation is distorted if it is carried outside the province of religion, and called in to explain phenomena of the physical or material order; the nature of faith is misunderstood if it is confused with a theoretical opinion and applied to the solving of problems which concern science alone.

This consideration, which rests on the direct testimony of Jesus, is so important that it seems to me to overshadow all the rest. If Protestant dogmatics are nothing short of the scientific expression of religious faith, if this faith itself has no other criterion but the

Gospel revelation, it is neither lawful nor right to erect into a dogma the tradition of the miraculous birth of Christ, and to invest the narratives which embody it with the religious authority of an article of faith.

There are still other reasons which forbid our entering upon this dangerous path and confusing the postulate enunciated by the Christian consciousness with the explanation attempted by popular belief. Let me merely offer three remarks, which traditional orthodoxy may have contested, but the value of which it has not been able to invalidate.

Do we not strike a blow at the essential character of Jesus, by explaining His divine sonship by means of His miraculous generation? by making the holiness (positive or negative) of Christ depend upon a material miracle? by reducing the divinity of the Saviour to a mystery effected in the bodily organism? Are we not lowering the moral and religious fact of His communion with God to the level of a physical process, which, doubtless, by the co-operation of the will of Jesus, must rise into the ethical sphere, but which nevertheless does not succeed in constituting a truly moral growth? Transformed into a dogma, the tradition of the miraculous birth marks the first stage in the doctrinal evolution which ends in a purely material conception of the divinity of Christ and of the Incarnation. Theology came to look upon the divinity and the humanity of Christ as two metaphysical substances, endowed with fixed properties and united in the person of Jesus by a supernatural act, deprived of all religious and moral character. Between the all too famous theory of the two natures and the physical notion of the origin of Christ, it would be easy to point out an antecedent agreement and affinities, singularly compromising for the theological solution which changed into a Scholastic dogma the naïve and poetic epic of early Christianity.

But the official doctrine not only lowers the notion of the Saviour's divinity in the material and physical sphere; it does away with His full and real humanity. If Jesus Christ is truly man, must He not be born in the same way as every other man?[1] When seriously considered, does not the traditional theory make Him a stranger to our race? The oft-invoked[2] analogy between the creation of the human race and the miraculous birth of Jesus is more apparent than real. It breaks down before the formidable difficulties raised by the historical character of the narrative in Genesis; it transfers the problem into a region surrounded by such impenetrable mysteries that all discussion is necessarily banished; it leaves the decision of the religious problem to be determined by the natural sciences, and makes Christian dogmatics the humble servant of physiology or of ethnography.

Finally, the orthodox conception labours under a dualism which proceeds from an ele-

[1] KEIM, *op. cit.*, ii. 53. BIEDERMANN, *Christliche Dogmatik*, § 582, 2. H. SCHULTZ, *op. cit.*, p. 394.

[2] See Note XXVII., p. 137.

mentary and superficial point of view; in its
endeavour to safeguard the divine character
and holy personality of the Saviour, it
draws a hard and fast line between what
we conventionally call nature and the supernatural.[1] It views the fact of the birth of
Christ as outside the ordinary working of
the divine activity in the laws of creation; it
tends to exclude the intervention of Providence
from the normal and regular play of the forces
of the physical and material world; it establishes an artificial hierarchy between regions
which are undistinguishable in the divine plan
of creation; it forgets that, for the Christian
filled with the Holy Spirit and who has thus
learnt to see God everywhere, this antinomy
is overcome and mastered[2]; it does not
believe that the new creation of the heavenly
Father's grace could have been effected under
the simple and divinely-ordained conditions of

[1] Read the judicious remarks of SCHLEIERMACHER in his
Second Letter to Lücke, Werke zur Theologie, Bd. II. pp.
618–619.

[2] See Note XXVIII., p. 138.

an ordinary birth; it can only value the un-
speakable gift, bestowed by heaven to earth,
at the price of a material and physical miracle.
Such are the claims of traditional theology;
I am aware that they are ultimately inspired
by faith, but it must be confessed that such
a faith comes perilously near to unbelief.

VI

To conclude. The official doctrine rests
upon the two narratives of Matthew and Luke
interpreted literally and raised into articles of
faith. The exegetical foundation of the dogma
does not bear the test of historical criticism.
The negative results obtained by the analysis
of the documents are completed and confirmed
by the positive conclusions yielded by Biblical
theology. In the light of this twofold investi-
gation the tradition of the miraculous birth of
Jesus vanishes away or rather resolves itself
into a myth created by popular devotion and
destined to explain the divine sonship of Christ

by His supernatural generation.[1] Thus viewed,
the conception of our two Evangelists is an
important landmark in the development of
Scriptural Christology ; if it ceases to remain
a real fact in the history of Jesus, it stands out
as the characteristic creation of the faith of the
Church.   But this faith is not bound up with
the form it assumed at the hands of the first
generations of Christians.   If we identify the
idea underlying this religious affirmation with
the merely symbolical expression of popular
poetry, we are courting unanswerable objections and insoluble difficulties.   Every
attempt made to reconstruct on a dogmatic
basis a notion now for ever overthrown by
exegesis and criticism, has but betrayed the in-
extricable contradictions of popular orthodoxy.
We are therefore doing a valuable service to
faith by confining the traditional doctrine to
its religious import.   By divesting the Christmas Gospel message of the dogmatic vesture

[1] Lipsius, *Die Bedeutung des Historischen im Christentum*,
in the work entitled *Glauben und Wissen*, 1897, p. 138.

in which it has been enclosed by ancient or modern Scholasticism, by laying bare the imperishable truth contained in the Christian symbol, we are remaining faithful to the mind of Jesus who bases His own unique communion with God not upon the physical miracle of His supernatural birth, but upon the sovereign election and perfect revelation of the heavenly Father (Matt. xi. 27). If we set aside the dogma which the school has deduced from the stories of Matthew and Luke, it is that we may subscribe with absolute sincerity and joyful assurance to the Johannine saying, echo of our experience and confirmation of our faith : " Jesus said unto them : I am from above ; I am not of this world."

Notes

Note I. to p. 34. " Such is the situation to-day, says M. Sabatier, that a man who professed to believe with his whole heart in Jesus Christ, as Son of God and Saviour, but confessed he could not decide whether the mode of His sonship was natural or supernatural, would be looked upon as an unfaithful member of the Church." A. SABATIER, *La Religion laïque*, Revue Chrétienne, t. xxix. [1882], p. 660. If I am not mistaken, this situation does not date from to-day ; it is as old as ecclesiastical orthodoxy.

Note II. to p. 34. *Symb. Apostol.* Credo . . . . in Jesum Christum . . . . qui conceptus est de Spiritu Sancto, natus ex Maria virgine

. . . . *Symb. nicaen.*, § 4 : . . . . Qui propter nos homines et propter nostram salutem descendit de cœlis, et incarnatus est de Spiritu sancto, ex Maria Virgine, et homo factus est . . . . *Conf. Aug.*, Art. III., §§ 1–2 : Docent, quod Verbum, hoc est Filius Dei, assumpserit humanam naturam in utero beatæ Mariæ Virginis. . . . Unus Christus, vere Deus et vere homo, natus ex virgine Maria. . . . *Conf. helvetica posterior*, Art. xi. : . . . . . Ex virgine Maria carnem assumpsit. . . . Eundem quoque æterni Dei æternum filium credimus et docemus hominis factum esse filium, ex semine Abrahæ atque Davidis, non ex viri coitu, quod Hebion dixit, sed conceptum purissime ex spiritu sancto, et natum ex Maria semper Virgine, sicut diligenter nobis historia explicat evangelica.—This dogma is the common inheritance of the Christian Churches; it is formulated in the œcumenical creeds and in the Protestant confessions, in the Roman Catechism and in the Socinian Catechism of Racow. As to the extent to which the Lutheran creeds have shared in the Catholic premisses of the official dogma, see below, § IV.

Note III. to p. 38.   Let me refer the reader to the most important works on the subject before us.   I do not pretend to have exhausted all the materials in giving the following refer-ences, but I think they will suffice to furnish every theologian with the means of becoming acquainted with all the elements of the discus-sion.   The conservative and apologetical School is most authoritatively represented by GODET's *Commentary on Saint Luke*, and by the *Life of Jesus* by WEISS.   We may also add STEIN-MEYER, *Die Geschichte der Geburt des Herrn und seiner ersten Schritte im Leben, mit Bezug auf die neueste Kritik*, 1873 ; NEBE, *Die Kindheitsgeschichte des Herrn nach Matthäus und Lukas*, 1893 ; A. BERTHOUD, *La nais-sance miraculeuse de Jesus-Christ* (Chrétien évangélique, 20 Mai 1893) ; A. THRAEN, *La naissance miraculeuse*.   (Paper read before the pastoral conference of Marseille, 1895, re-printed in the author's posthumous *Confér-*

ences apologétiques et dogmatiques, Paris, 1900, pp. 51–161); GORE, *Dissertations on subjects connected with the Incarnation*, 1896², pp. 1–68, The Virgin Birth of our Lord ; GORE, *The Incarnation of the Son of God*, Bampton Lectures, 1891, London, 1898¹⁰ ; SANDAY, *The Virgin Birth of our Lord Jesus Christ*. (Christian World Pulpit, 4 February 1903).— J. A. ROBINSON, *Some Thoughts on the Incarnation*, 1903.—The historical and critical School is represented and voiced by the *Lives of Jesus* by STRAUSS and KEIM, and, on the special subject before us, by BEYSCHLAG, the *Commentaries on the Gospels*, by DE WETTE, REUSS, HOLTZMANN ; SYDOW, *Die wunderbare Geburt Jesu*, Berlin, 1873 ; *Aktenstücke betreffend das über mich verhängte Disciplinarverfahren wegen meines Vortrags über die wunderbare Geburt Jesu*, Berlin, 1873 ; F. FISCHER, *Das Berliner Consistorium und Sydow*, Berlin, 1873 ; HILLMANN, *Die Kindheitsgeschichte Jesu nach Lukas* (Jahrbücher für protestantische Theologie, 1891, 192–

261); USENER, *Religionsgeschichtliche Unter-suchungen*, Band I., Bonn, 1889; ROHRBACH, *Geboren von der Jungfrau*. Das Zeugniss des Neuen Testaments gegen die Lehre von der übernatürlichen Geburt Jesu Christi, Berlin, 1898[4]; HERING, *Die dogmatische Bedeutung und der religiöse Wert der über-natürlichen Geburt Christi* (Zeitschrift für Theologie und Kirche, herausgegeben von Gottschick, Jahrgang V., 1895, pp. 58–91); SOLTAU, *Die Geburtsgeschichte Jesu Christi*, Leipzig, 1902. The heated controversy in Germany, about ten years ago, over the so-called Apostles' Creed, often bore upon the dogma of the miraculous birth, and gave rise to a certain number of works immediately inspired by the controversy. The following books issued from the apologetic and dogmatic camp: WOHLENBERG, *Empfangen von heili-gen Geist, geboren von der Jungfrau Maria*, Leipzig, 1893; WAGNER, *Mitteilungen und Nachrichten für die evangelische Kirche in Russland*, Januarheft, 1894. *Cf.* HAUSSLEITER,

Zur Vorgeschichte des apostolischen Glaubens-bekenntnisses, München, 1893 ; and especially TH. ZAHN, *Das apostolische Symbolum*, Erlangen and Leipzig, 1893. CREMER, *Zum Kampf um das Apostolikum*, 1892. The theses defended by these writers have met with serious opponents : HARNACK, *The Apostles' Creed*, 1892 ; HERRMANN, *Worum handelt es sich im dem Streit um das Apostolikum?* Leipzig, 1893 ; BORNEMANN, *Der Streit um das Apostolikum*, Magdeburg, 1893 ; KATTENBUSCH, *Das apostolische Symbol*, 2 vols., Leipzig, 1894, 1897, 1900.—*Cf.* HARNACK, *History of Dogma*, vol. I.—HOLTZMANN, in his Handbook of Biblical Theology, has given, with admirable clearness and conciseness, a summary of the exegetical and historical discussions to which the problem gave rise ; bibliographical information, as ample as exact, will also be found in the chapter, *Lehrbuch der neutestamentlichen Theologie*, 1897, vol. i. pp. 409–415.

Note IV. to p. 41. *Cf.* GODET's admission, *Commentary on the Gospel of St. Luke*, i.

(1875), p. 158. I shall often have occasion to refer to the author's general conclusions on chapters i. and ii. of that Gospel. The third edition (1888), vol. i. pp. 212-224, does not differ from the second in its main ideas; but as the latter (i. 151-204) is richer in details than the last edition, I shall adhere to the work of 1875.

Note V. to p. 43. Observe in the Lives of Jesus and in the Commentaries " l'échafaudage de combinaisons " (GODET, i. 252) the elaborate contrivances imagined by harmonizers to elude these difficulties. Why should we find GODET and WEISS among the champions of the view which, in spite of the most elementary laws of grammar and philology, maintains that the genealogy preserved by Luke comes from Mary, and not Joseph? Compare, as against the interpretation of WEISS, the judicious remarks of HAUPT (*Theologische Studien und Kritiken*, 1884, pp. 56-57). It is well to note that the evidence of the historical facts has strongly impressed some of the theologians of the traditional school, who, like the representatives of the historical school, admit that both our Gospels give the genealogy of Joseph (HOFMANN, DELITZSCH, FRANK); THOMASIUS confesses himself uncertain and perplexed (*Christi Person und Werk*, ii., 1857, p. 129). As a harmonizer, THRAEN displays a skill which is perhaps superior to that of the older apologists ; nevertheless we may justly affirm that he is not more successful than his predecessors. See *op. cit.*, pp. 57–119.

Note VI. to p. 49. RÉVILLE, *op. cit.*, p. 27 ; REUSS, *op. cit.*, p. 157. Is criticism, so abused by GODET, wrong in detecting in Luke ii. 33 ("his father and his mother"), ii. 27 and 43 ("his parents"), the remains of a conception identical to the one set forth in the genealogies ? This hypothesis is supported by the fact that the copyists have here indulged in characteristic alterations; whereas the best authorities favour the reading οὐκ ἔγνωσαν οἱ γονεῖς αὐτοῦ, a few manuscripts

bear οὐκ ἔγνω Ἰωσὴφ καὶ ἡ μήτηρ αὐτοῦ.
ROHRBACH (*op. cit.*) attaches the utmost importance to the recent discovery of a fragment
of a Syriac translation of the New Testament,
probably dating from the second century ; it
concludes the genealogical list in Matthew
thus : *Jacob begat Joseph, Joseph (to whom the
Virgin Mary was betrothed) begat Jesus who
is called Christ.* However, the antiquity of
this manuscript is disputed, and it is impossible
to estimate its historical character and value.
See G. PASCAL, Revue de Théologie de Mont-
auban, 1st July 1895.   (*Un nouveau manuscrit
syriaque*) ; THRAEN, *op. cit.*, p. 83 *et seq.* ;
HOLZBERG, *Der neuentdeckte Codex Syrus
Sinaiticus*, 1896.

Note VII. to p. 51.   *Cf.* HASE, *Geschichte
Jesu*, Leipzig, 1876, p. 184.—John vii. 5 :
"For even his brethren did not believe on
him." Nothing warrants our attributing to
the brethren of Jesus alone the intentions
spoken of by Mark, and maintaining that the
mother of Jesus was yielding to a feeling of

anxiety and a desire to prevent the conflict which she foresaw (GODET, i. 157). *Cf.* THRAEN, *op. cit.*, pp. 92–98.

Note VIII. to p. 52. Whatever explanation may be given of the participle ὁρισθέντος, the whole context, no less than the term σπέρμα, is unfavourable to the idea of supernatural generation. REUSS, *Histoire de la théologie chrétienne au siècle apostolique*, ii. (3rd edit.), 1864, pp. 70–71.—With reference to the whole of this part, consult HOLTZMANN's study, *Die paulinische Christologie im Verhältniss zu dem Gegensatz von σάρξ und πνεῦμα* (Zeitschrift für wissenschaftliche Theologie, 1888, especially pp. 280–283). HOLTZMANN, *Zur paulinischen Praeexistenzlehre* (same Review, 1884, p. 132). A. SABATIER, *The Apostle Paul*, pp. 314–315. "The position that this fact (supernatural birth) occupies in ecclesiastical theology is filled in the Apostle's system by that of the resurrection. The new epoch of history begins with the Saviour's resurrection, which was the first manifestation of the *spiritual*

life on earth." The apologetical remarks of
HAUSSLEITER (*op. cit.*, 36) and of THRAEN
(105–109) in no way weaken the arguments
adduced above.

Note IX. to p. 55. That is to say, the
fourth Gospel and the so-called epistles of
John. As regards the Apocalypse, on two
occasions we find it using a term implying
natural descent and ordinary filiation. V. 5:
ἡ ῥίζα Δαυίδ ; xxii. 16 : ἐγώ εἰμι ἡ ῥίζα καὶ
τὸ γένος Δαυίδ.—BIEDERMANN argues that the
passage Apoc. xii. 13 may have contributed
to the growth of the myth in the Gospel
(*Christliche Dogmatik*, § 582, 9); but that is
a conjecture the likelihood of which is partly
bound up with the view one holds as to
the origin and literary composition of the
Apocalypse.

Note X. to p. 57. A. SABATIER, *Encyclopédie des sciences religieuses*, vii. 363.—H.
SCHULTZ sees in John i. 13 an indirect refuta-
tion of any opinion which founds the divine
filiation upon a physical miracle. In the eyes

of religious faith, which postulates the divine origin of the personality of Christ, the son of God is ἀμήτωρ as well as ἀπάτωρ, Heb. vii. 3. (*Die Lehre von der Gottheit Christi*, Gotha, 1881, p. 459; *cf.* p. 391.) With SCHULTZ, STRAUSS holds that the Johannine theory of the Logos precludes the notion of the supernatural birth. (*Das Leben Jesu kritisch bearbeitet*, 1835, i. 155.)

Note XI. to p. 62. "Had the birth of Jesus been illegitimate, as later on the opponents of Christianity actually hinted, his personal enemies in Galilee, especially at Nazareth where he was less admired and loved than elsewhere, would not have failed to have reproached him with it, and we should find some slight traces of the fact even in the pages of his own historians." A. RÉVILLE, *op. cit.*, p. 27. *Cf.* STRAUSS, *Das Leben Jesu kritisch bearbeitet*, 1835, Bd. I., § 28; *id.*, *Die christliche Glaubenslehre*, ii. 94–95.

Note XII. to p. 64. A more exhaustive study of the scriptural theses as to the pre-existence of Christ is not part of my present subject; may I refer the reader to my essay on the *Notion de la préexistence du Fils de Dieu*, Paris, 1883, and to the second of my *Études sur la méthode de la dogmatique protestante* (Revue de Théologie et de Philosophie, 1885, pp. 473–498 ; 571–601). Recent research has valuably confirmed the solution I there tried to put forth and defend. BALDENSPERGER, *Die messianisch - apocalyptischen Hoffnungen des Judentums*, 1903, pp. 144–151. FRANKE, *Die neutestamentlichen Grundlagen der Lehre von der Praeexistenz Christi*, (Theol. Stud. u. Krit., 1887, § 323–352). HARNACK, *Notions of pre-existence and their application to the Messiah*. History of Dogma, i. 102 and 318. MOHNHAUPT, *Historische Entwickelung und dogmatische Darstellung der Lehre von der Praeexistenz Christi* (Jahrbücher für protestantische Theologie, 1888, 161–209). HOLTZMANN, *op. cit.*, i. 338–9 ; 405–409 ; ii. 81–87 *sq.*, 296–311, 401–404. On the opposite side, see CORDEY, *La foi à la pré-*

existence de Jesus-Christ et son importance pour la piété chrétienne, 1893.

Note XIII. to p. 66. In assigning this place to the attempted solution on the part of the " Gospels of the infancy," I do not intend to commit myself on the chronological question of the origin of the myth itself; all I mean to say is that from the point of view of dogmatic thought, the theory consecrated by Matthew and Luke is inferior to the speculative thesis of the pre-existence. *Cf.* SCHULTZ, *Die Lehre von der Gottheit Christi*, Gotha, 1881, pp. 391–392.

Note XIV. to p. 67. A. RÉVILLE, *Histoire du dogme de la divinité de Jésus-Christ*, Paris, 1869, p. 29: " The meaning which we place upon this particular aspect of the first Christian legend is so consonant with the mind and the methods of the times that, in the fraction of Christendom in which Jesus was still looked upon as the son of Joseph, the Holy Spirit, a feminine word in Hebrew, was made, not the generator, but the *Mother* of

Jesus : ἡ μήτηρ μοῦ τὸ ἅγιον πνεῦμα, my mother the Holy Spirit, says Jesus in the Gospel of the Hebrews." (Quoted by ORIGEN, *Homil. in Jerem.*, xv., ed. LOM-MATZSCH, t. xv. p. 284.)

Note XV. to p. 71. " From his mother's womb." The religious writers among the Jews loved to use this expression when they meant to signify that a good or bad quality originated as far back as possible in a person's life, was born, so to speak, with that person. Thus Job (xxxi. 18) calls himself a protector of the widow and orphan from his mother's womb, and the Psalmist (li. 5) declares himself a sinner from the moment of his birth. A. RÉVILLE, *Histoire du dogme de la divinité de Jésus-Christ*, Paris, 1869, p. 29.

Note XVI. to p. 75. I confidently trust that after the preceding exposition the term *myth* will no longer give rise to the misapprehensions which an orthodoxy divested of intelligence and a rationalism bereft of the religious sense have equally contributed to propagate and

Note XXVI. to p. 102. I make bold to think that on the ground of this religious affirmation an understanding is possible with the representatives of contemporary orthodoxy. See the valuable remark of GODET, *op. cit.*, i. 161, on KEIM's solution, *History of Jesus of Nazara*, ii. 63 *sq.*: "While holding the paternal concurrence in the birth of this extraordinary man, he admits a divine interposition which profoundly influenced and completely sanctified the appearance of this Being. This attempt at explanation is a homage rendered to the incomparable moral greatness of Jesus, and we think it leaves untouched the great object of faith—Jesus Christ's dignity as the Saviour." *Cf.* SCHLEIERMACHER, *Der christliche Glaube*, § 97; H. SCHULTZ, *op. cit.*, 392–393; BEYSCHLAG, *op. cit.*, i. 169; HAUPT, *Theolog. Stud. und Krit.*, 1884, pp. 58–59. THRAEN, 160–161.—We entirely accept the reproach directed by STRAUSS (*Die christliche Glaubenslehre*, ii. 97–98) against SCHLEIERMACHER, a reproach which finally amounts to the accusa-

tion of having attributed to Christ a sovereign
and incomparable dignity, and of having exalted
Him above the common level of humanity. It
seems to us that the general considerations
by means of which LUTHARDT attempts to
establish the fact of the supernatural birth
of Christ (*Apologetische Vorträge*, Bd. II[3].,
1871, pp. 73-75, 256) are not incompatible
with the opinion which I am trying to
defend.

Note XXVII. to p. 108. See, for example,
GODET, *op. cit.*, i. 161.—In his *Biblical Studies*
(N.T., 1876, p. 89) GODET seems to have felt
the weakness of this objection, for he adds this
significant note: " This would still remain
true, even if we granted the Darwinian hypothesis, which, taken in its utmost strictness,
still only applies to the body of man, not to
his soul, unless indeed we are willing to give
up, in the case of man, the distinctive feature
of his being — his moral freedom." What
could be more superficial than this external
and abstract dualism established by the older

psychology between the mind and the physical organism !

Note **XXVIII.** to p. 109. A. SABATIER, *La Religion laïque* (*Revue chrétienne*, t. xxix. [1882], pp. 660-661. " For the Christian, God is in what the ordinary man calls nature, and also in the region which he proclaims above nature. Religious unity, restored in his own consciousness, reveals itself likewise in the universal course of creation. He does not deny the extraordinary facts of which history assures him, but he learns to look upon them in another light as proceeding from the very depths of the eternal creation of God, and not as later additions from without. For him nature and the supernatural are reconciled and united in the very plan of divine creation."

PRINTED BY NEILL AND CO., LTD., EDINBURGH.

Jesus : ἡ μήτηρ μοῦ τὸ ἅγιον πνεῦμα, my mother the Holy Spirit, says Jesus in the Gospel of the Hebrews." (Quoted by ORIGEN, *Homil. in Jerem.*, xv., ed. LOMMATZSCH, t. xv. p. 284.)

Note XV. to p. 71. "From his mother's womb." The religious writers among the Jews loved to use this expression when they meant to signify that a good or bad quality originated as far back as possible in a person's life, was born, so to speak, with that person. Thus Job (xxxi. 18) calls himself a protector of the widow and orphan from his mother's womb, and the Psalmist (li. 5) declares himself a sinner from the moment of his birth. A. RÉVILLE, *Histoire du dogme de la divinité de Jésus-Christ*, Paris, 1869, p. 29.

Note XVI. to p. 75. I confidently trust that after the preceding exposition the term *myth* will no longer give rise to the misapprehensions which an orthodoxy divested of intelligence and a rationalism bereft of the religious sense have equally contributed to propagate and popularize. Myth, no less than history, can serve as a means and channel of revelation from above, and some of the profoundest conceptions of the Old and New Testaments have found their way to hearts and consciences in the garb of symbols containing immortal and divine truths. *Cf.* H. SCHULTZ, *Alttestamentliche Theologie*, Introduction, chap. iii. § 3.

Note XVII. to p. 75. *Cf.* STRAUSS, *op. cit.*, i. 174–175; HASE, *Geschichte Jesu*, 1876, 197–200. ORIGEN had already laid great stress on the mythological analogies to be found in the religions of classical paganism as an argument in favour of the miraculous birth. See *Contra Celsum*, i. 37; *Princ.*, ii. 6. *Cf.* CLEMENT OF ALEXANDRIA, *Paedag.*, i. 6. Before these, even JUSTIN, *Apol.*, i. 21. In a work of the highest interest, but wherein the method applied to the documents of the Bible is supremely defective (*Religionsgeschichtliche Untersuchungen*, Erster Theil: *Das Weihnachtsfest*, Bonn, 1889), USENER has accumulated a series of data (see especially pp. 70–76) containing remarkable likenesses to our Gospel tradition. Yet the conclusions which he draws from them go singularly beyond his premisses: the Jewish and Christian factors suffice to explain the genesis of the myth of the nativity. This has been admirably shewn by HARNACK in his reply to USENER (*Theol. Literaturzeitung*, 1889, No. 8; see principally col. 204-5). SOLTAU, *op. cit.*, brings forward analogies borrowed from classical antiquity. ROHRBACH, *op. cit.*, goes back to the legend of the Bouddha. HARNACK's remarks apply equally to these two authors. At most it might be argued that the physical notion of the divine filiation of Jesus perhaps gained rapid currency in pagan-Christian communities, because minds were there prepared for such an explanation by the analogies which the Fathers of the Church themselves pointed out (*cf.* HOLTZMANN, *Hand - Commentar zum Neuen Testament*, I. Band, Freiburg i. B., 1889, p. 32). Moreover, USENER has just retracted a considerable number of his previous assertions, in a study which takes into fuller account the works of theologians on the question he is treating: *Geburt und Kindheit Jesu* (Zeit-schrift für neutestamentliche Wissenschaft, 1903, p. 1–21).

Note XVIII. to p. 76. A considerable number of theologians think that the Gospel myth partly owes its origin to the very wide-spread bias in favour of the religious and moral superiority of virginity; they remind us that the asceticism which extols celibacy at the expense of marriage is found in the Apocryphal books of the Old Testament, among the Essenes, in Philo, in the Epistles of the apostle Paul (1 Cor. vii.), and in the Apocalypse (xiv. 4), and that it very early passed into the Christian Church, under the pressure of Oriental and Hellenic influences (*cf.* KEIM, *op. cit.*, ii. 60; BALDENSPERGER cites the Talmudic legends about the virginity of the mother of Moses, *Das Selbstbewusstsein Jesu im Lichte der messianischen Hoffnungen seiner Zeit*, 1888, p. 117). It is not impossible that the tradition of the supernatural birth was formed in an environment in which such ideas were current : this opinion is held, for example, by CHAPUIS, *Annales de bibliographie théologique*, 1896, p. 119.   Yet the ascetic glorification of celibacy, unknown to the Old Testament, seems equally absent from our Gospel documents, and there is no trace of it in the passages which mention the parents and family of Jesus : Matt. i. 25 ; Luke ii. 7 ; Matt. xii. 46 ; Luke viii. 19.   (*Cf.* WEISS, *op. cit.*, i. 220.)

Note XIX. to p. 82.   This has been noticed by theologians holding the official doctrine, for example, WEISS, *Life of Christ*, i. 257. — SCHLEIERMACHER had already drawn attention to this point (*Der christliche Glaube*, § 97, 2).—It is not without reason that the parallelism between the message of the angel (Luke i. 35) and the beginning of the story of the creation (Gen. i. 2) has been pointed out. THOMASIUS, *op. cit.*, ii. 129–130.

Note XX. to p. 85.   H. SCHULTZ (*Die Lehre von der Gottheit Christi*, Gotha, 1881,

p. 393) rightly reminds us that, according to the Biblical conception, woman is represented as weaker and more open than man to the temptations which come from the instincts of natural selfishness (Gen. iii.; Eccl. vii.; 1 Tim. ii. 14).

Note XXI. to p. 86. *Cf.* GODET, *op. cit.*, i. 93–94; WENNAGEL, *La logique des disciples de Ritschl et la logique de la Kénose*, 1883, p. 58. THRAEN, *op. cit.*, pp. 132–135. See the retort of BIEDERMANN (*Christliche Dogmatik*, § 582, Anm. 1) to SCHENKEL, *Die christliche Dogmatik vom Standpunkte des Gewissens aus dargestellt*, Band II. (Wiesbaden, 1859), p. 732 *sq.* *Cf.* GESS, *Das Dogma von Christi Person und Werk entwickelt aus Christi Selbstzeugniss und dem Zeugniss der Apostel*, Basel, 1887, pp. 364–366.

Note XXII. to p. 88. STRAUSS, *Die christliche Glaubenslehre*, ii. 90 *sq.*, has traced with merciless rigour the history of the problems which theology has raised in connection with the dogma of the miraculous conception

of Christ; he has shewn how the leaven of
the Catholicism of the Fathers has penetrated
even into Protestant doctrine, seeing that
two creeds of the Lutheran Church teach, like
the Roman creed, the perpetual and perfect
virginity of Mary. *Art. Smalc.*, i. 4 : Filius
ita factus est homo, ut a spiritu sancto sine
virili opera conciperetur, et ex Maria pura,
sancta, semper virgine nasceretur. *Form. Conc.*
(*Solid. declar.*, viii. 24) : De virgine, inviolata
ipsius virginitate, natus est, unde et vere
θεοτόκος, Dei genitrix est, et tamen virgo
mansit. *Cf.* LUTHER, edit. Erl., xxii. 18.
ZWINGLI, *Fidei Ratio*: ex immaculata per-
petuaque virgine Maria; *Fidei Expositio*:
ejusdem perpetuo servata virginitate. *Con-
fessio helvetica posterior*, Art. xi. : conceptum
purissime ex spiritu sancto, et natum ex Maria
semper Virgine. *Cf. Basileensis prior*, Disp.
8–9.

Note XXIII. to p. 90. RÉVILLE, *op. cit.*,
p. 30 : "A pre-existing being who becomes
man lowers himself, if you will, to the level of

a human embryo ; but he is not *conceived* by
virtue of an act external to himself, in the
womb of a woman. The conception is the
moment when an individual is formed who
had no previous existence, at least as an individual. Where, on the contrary, pre-existence or incarnation is postulated, in Paul and
John for example, no mention is made of a
miraculous conception." HARNACK, *History
of Dogma*, vol. i. HOLTZMANN, *op. cit.*, ii. 417.

Note XXIV. to p. 92. IRENÆUS may
be looked upon as the first exponent of this
theory. His idea of a *recapitulation* or new
beginning presents striking analogies with the
doctrine of our modern speculators, iii. 20–21 ;
iii. 22, 4 ; v. 19, 1 ; v. 21, 1. ROTHE and
DORNER are the most distinguished exponents
of this theory. *Cf.* ROTHE, *Theologische
Ethik*, § 533 (t. iii., 1870), p. 135 *sq. Dogmatik*, herausgegeben von SCHENKEL, ii. 180
sq. ; *Stille Stunden*, p. 279 *sq.*—DORNER,
System der christlichen Glaubenslehre, Berlin,
1881, ii. 446–451. LANGE, *Christl. Dogmatik*,

vi. 644.—*Cf.* CH. SECRÉTAN, *La Raison et le
Christianisme*, 1863, pp. 259, et 277 (quoted by
GODET, *op. cit.*, i. 160). If I have rightly
understood the obscure and artificial deduc-
tions of FRANK, *System der christlichen Wahr-
heit*, Erlangen II. (1880), p. 106, he too must
be ranked among the partisans of the doctrine
described and discussed here.

Note XXV. to p. 94. *Cf.* COLANI, *De la
personne de Jésus-Christ. Essai d'une christologie positive*, Revue de Théologie, t. xi.,
Strasbourg, 1855, p. 108. The uselessness of
the dogma of the miraculous birth of Christ
seems so evident to COLANI that he does not
stop to prove its uselessness. But COLANI has
omitted to bring out the positive interest and
religious motive of the traditional doctrine.
His criticism is incomplete because it is purely
negative. The first article on Christology by
COLANI, *Étude critique des systèmes ortho-
doxes* (t. x. pp. 349–370) nowhere treats of
the dogma of the miraculous birth of
Christ.

Note XXVI. to p. 102. I make bold to think that on the ground of this religious affirmation an understanding is possible with the representatives of contemporary orthodoxy. See the valuable remark of GODET, *op. cit.*, i. 161, on KEIM's solution, *History of Jesus of Nazara*, ii. 63 *sq.* : "While holding the paternal concurrence in the birth of this extraordinary man, he admits a divine interposition which profoundly influenced and completely sanctified the appearance of this Being. This attempt at explanation is a homage rendered to the incomparable moral greatness of Jesus, and we think it leaves untouched the great object of faith—Jesus Christ's dignity as the Saviour." *Cf.* SCHLEIERMACHER, *Der christliche Glaube*, § 97 ; H. SCHULTZ, *op. cit.*, 392–393 ; BEYSCHLAG, *op. cit.*, i. 169; HAUPT, *Theolog. Stud. und Krit.*, 1884, pp. 58–59. THRAEN, 160–161.—We entirely accept the reproach directed by STRAUSS (*Die christliche Glaubenslehre*, ii. 97–98) against SCHLEIERMACHER, a reproach which finally amounts to the accusa-

tion of having attributed to Christ a sovereign
and incomparable dignity, and of having exalted
Him above the common level of humanity. It
seems to us that the general considerations
by means of which LUTHARDT attempts to
establish the fact of the supernatural birth
of Christ (*Apologetische Vorträge*, Bd. II⁸.,
1871, pp. 73–75, 256) are not incompatible
with the opinion which I am trying to
defend.

Note XXVII. to p. 108.   See, for example,
GODET, *op. cit.*, i. 161.—In his *Biblical Studies*
(N.T., 1876, p. 89) GODET seems to have felt
the weakness of this objection, for he adds this
significant note: "This would still remain
true, even if we granted the Darwinian hypothesis, which, taken in its utmost strictness,
still only applies to the body of man, not to
his soul, unless indeed we are willing to give
up, in the case of man, the distinctive feature
of his being — his moral freedom." What
could be more superficial than this external
and abstract dualism established by the older

psychology between the mind and the physical organism!

Note XXVIII. to p. 109. A. SABATIER, *La Religion laïque* (*Revue chrétienne*, t. xxix. [1882], pp. 660–661. "For the Christian, God is in what the ordinary man calls nature, and also in the region which he proclaims above nature. Religious unity, restored in his own consciousness, reveals itself likewise in the universal course of creation. He does not deny the extraordinary facts of which history assures him, but he learns to look upon them in another light as proceeding from the very depths of the eternal creation of God, and not as later additions from without. For him nature and the supernatural are reconciled and united in the very plan of divine creation."

PRINTED BY NEILL AND CO., LTD., EDINBURGH.